KU-576-263

BECAUSE WE SAY SO

NOAM CHOMSKY

HAMISH HAMILTON
an imprint of
PENGUIN BOOKS

HAMISH HAMILTON

UK | USA | Canada | Ireland | Australia
India | New Zealand | South Africa

Hamish Hamilton is part of the Penguin Random House group of companies
whose addresses can be found at global.penguinrandomhouse.com.

First published in the United States of America by City Lights Books 2015
First published in Great Britain by Hamish Hamilton 2015
001

Text copyright © Noam Chomsky, 2015
Foreword copyright © Henry A. Giroux, 2015

The moral right of the authors has been asserted

The writings in this book are adapted from essays
by Noam Chomsky distributed by The New York Times Syndicate.

Printed in Great Britain by Clays Ltd, St Ives plc

A CIP catalogue record for this book is available from the British Library

HARDBACK ISBN: 978-0-241-18835-4
TRADE PAPERBACK ISBN: 978-0-241-18836-1

Because We Say So

Photograph copyright © Don J. Usner, 2010

Noam Chomsky is the author of numerous bestselling and influential political books, including *Hegemony or Survival*, *Failed States*, *Interventions*, *What We Say Goes*, *Hopes and Prospects*, *Gaza in Crisis*, *Making the Future*, *Occupy* and *On Palestine*.

Henry A. Giroux currently holds the Global TV Network Chair Professorship at McMaster University in the English and Cultural Studies Department and a Distinguished Visiting Professorship at Ryerson University. His most recent books include *The Violence of Organized Forgetting* and *Disposable Futures: The Seduction of Violence in the Age of Spectacle*, co-written with Brad Evans.

CONTENTS

NOAM CHOMSKY AND THE PUBLIC INTELLECTUAL IN TURBULENT TIMES

By Henry A. Giroux

World-renowned academic Noam Chomsky is best known not only for his pioneering work in linguistics but also for his ongoing work as a public intellectual, in which he addresses numerous important social issues that include and often connect oppressive foreign and domestic policies—a fact well illustrated throughout this important collection of his recent political columns, *BECAUSE WE SAY SO*.

Chomsky's role intellectually, educationally and politically is more relevant now than ever given the need for a display of civic courage, theoretical rigor, and willingness to translate oppression and suffering into public concerns. Moreover, he provides a model for young people and others to understand the importance of using ideas and knowledge to intervene in civic, political and cultural life making it clear that democracy has to be struggled over, if it is going to survive.

Chomsky's political interventions have been historically specific while continually building on the power relations he has engaged critically. For instance, his initial ideas about the responsibility of intellectuals cannot be separated from his early criticisms of the Vietnam War and the complicity of intellectuals in brokering and legitimating that horrendous act of military intervention.[1] Yet, while it might appear difficult to compare his 1988 book, *MANUFACTURING CONSENT*, coauthored with Edward S. Herman, with his 2002 bestseller, 9/11, what all of his texts share is a luminous theoretical, political and forensic analysis of the functioning of the current global power structure, new and old modes of oppressive authority, and the ways in which neoliberal economic and social policies have produced more savage forms of global domination and corporate sovereignty. That uncompromising analysis is present on every page of *BECAUSE WE SAY SO*.

Each column in this book confirms that Chomsky does not subscribe to a one-dimensional notion of power that one often finds among many on the left. He keenly understands that power is multifaceted, operating through a number of material and symbolic registers, and he is particularly astute in pointing out that power also has a pedagogical function and must include a historical understanding of the public relations industry and of existing and emerging cultural apparatuses, and that central to matters of power, agency and the radical imagination are modes of persuasion, the shaping of identities, and the molding of desire.

Chomsky incessantly exposes the gap between the reality and the promise of a radical democracy, particularly in the United States, though he often provides detailed analysis of how the deformation of democracy works in a number of countries that hide their diverse modes of oppression behind the false claims of democratization. Chomsky has attempted to both refigure the promise of democracy and develop new ways to theorize agency and the social imagination outside of the neoliberal focus on individualization, privatization and the assumption that the only value that matters is exchange value. Unlike many intellectuals who are trapped in the discourse of academic silos and a sclerotic professionalism, he writes and speaks from the perspective of what might be called contingent totalities. In so doing, he connects a wide variety of issues as part of a larger understanding of the diverse and specific economic, social and political forces that shape people's lives at particular historical conjunctures. He is one of the few North American theorists who embrace modes of solidarity and collective struggle less as an afterthought than as central to what it means to connect the civic, social and ethical as the foundation for global resistance movements. Implicit to his role as a public intellectual are the questions of what a real democracy should look like, how its ideals and practices are subverted, and what forces are necessary to bring it into being. These are the questions at the heart of his thinking, his talks and the commentaries in this book.

For Chomsky, crises are viewed as overlapping, merging into each other in ways that often go unrecognized. In fact, Chomsky often brings together in his work issues such as terrorism, corporate power, American exceptionalism and other major concerns so as to provide maps that enable his readers to refigure the landscape of political, cultural and social life in ways that offer up new connections and the possibility for fresh modes of theorizing potential resistance.

He has also written about the possibility of political and economic alternatives, offering a fresh language for a collective sense of agency and resistance, a new understanding of the commons, and a rewriting of the relations between the political and the up-to-date institutions of culture, finance and capital. And yet he does not provide recipes but speaks to emerging modes of imaginative resistance always set within the boundaries of specific historical conjunctures. His work is especially important in understanding the necessity of public intellectuals in times of tyranny, cruelty, financial savagery and increasing authoritarianism. His work should be required reading for all academics, students and the wider public. That he is one of the most cited intellectuals in the world strongly suggest that his audience is general, diverse and widespread, inhabiting many different sites, public spheres and locations.

Chomsky is fiercely critical of fashionable conservative and liberal attempts to divorce intellectual activities from politics and is quite frank in his notion that education both in and out of institutional schooling should be involved in the practice of freedom and not just the pursuit of truth. He has strongly argued that educators, artists, journalists and other intellectuals have a responsibility to provide students and the wider public the knowledge and skills they need to be able to learn how to think rigorously, to be self-reflective and to develop the capacity to govern rather than be governed. But for Chomsky it is not enough to learn how to think critically. Engaged intellectuals must also develop an ethical imagination and sense of social responsibility necessary to make power accountable and to deepen the possibilities for everyone to live dignified lives infused with freedom, liberty, decency, care and justice.

On higher education, Chomsky has been arguing since the 1960s that in a healthy society, universities must press the claims for economic and social justice and that any education that matters must be not merely critical but also subversive. Chomsky has been unflinching in his belief that education should disturb the peace and engage in the production of knowledge that is critical of the status quo, particularly in a time of legitimized violence. He has also been clear, as were his late political counterparts, Pierre Bourdieu and Edward Said, in asserting that intellectuals had to make their voices accessible to a wider public and be heard in all of those spheres of public life in which there is an ongoing struggle over knowledge, values, power, identity, agency and the social imagination.

Capitalism may have found an honored place for many of its anti-public intellectuals, but it certainly has no room for the likes of Chomsky. Conservatives and liberals, along with an army of unyielding neoliberal advocates, have virtually refused to include him in the many discussions and publications on social issues that work their way into the various registers of the dominant media. In many ways, Chomsky's role as an intellectual and activist is a prototype of what may be called an American radical tradition. Despite this, Chomsky appears to be an exile in his own country by virtue of his constant dissent, the shock of his acts of translation, and his displays of fierce courage. Evidence of this is in your hands. The commentaries presented in this book are a collection of columns penned between 2011 and 2014, distributed to the international press by the New York Times Syndicate, and widely published in newspapers abroad. Few, if any, are published on the op-ed pages of American papers, and U.S. military censors even banned distribution of an earlier collection of his commentaries, *INTERVENTIONS*.[2]

As an engaged academic, Chomsky publicly argues against regimes of domination organized for the production of violence, and social and civil death. The force of his presence—his relentless speaking schedule and torrent of writing—offers up the possibility of dangerous memories, alternative ways of imagining society and the future, and the necessity of public criticism as one important element of individual and collective resistance. And yet Chomsky's role as a public intellectual, given the huge audiences that he attracts when he lectures as well as his large reading public, suggests that there is no politics that matters without a sense of connecting meaningfully with others. Politics becomes emancipatory when it takes seriously that, as Stuart Hall has noted, "People have to invest something of themselves, something that they recognize is of them or speaks to their condition, and without that moment of recognition . . . politics will go on, but you won't have a political movement without that moment of identification."[3] Chomsky clearly connects with a need among the public for those intellectuals willing to make power visible, to offer an alternative understanding of the world, and to point to the hopes of a future that does not imitate the scurrilous present.

Chomsky has been relentless in reminding society that power takes many forms and that the production of ignorance is not merely about the crisis of test scores or a natural state of affairs, but about how ignorance is often produced in the service of power. According to Chomsky, ignorance is a pedagogical formation that is used to stifle thinking and promotes a form of anti-politics, which undermines matters of judgment and thoughtfulness central to politics. At the same time, it is a crucial factor not just in producing consent but also in squelching dissent. For Chomsky, ignorance is a political weapon that benefits the powerful, not a general condition rooted in some inexplicable human condition.

In one of his many examples throughtout the book, he points to the efforts of the financial elite and their marketing machines to atomize people so they will be complicit in the destruction of the commons. Drawing on his expansive understanding of history, Chomsky cites the political economist Thorstein Veblen's emphasis on "fabricating wants" in order to not only manufacture ignorance but also define consumption as the major force in shaping their needs. For Chomsky, historical memory and individual and social agency are under attack, and this is as much a pedagogical as a political issue.

One of Chomsky's most insistent themes focuses on how state power functions in various forms as a mode of terrorism inflicting violence, misery and hardship, often as a function of class warfare and American global imperialism, and how people are often complicit with such acts of barbarism.

At the same time, Chomsky is also an ardent defender of the impoverished, those communities considered disposable, the excluded, and those marginalized by class, race, gender and other ideologies and structural relations considered dangerous to tyrants both at home and abroad. Yet there is no privileged, singularly oppressed group in Chomsky's work. He is capacious in making visible and interrogating oppression in its multiple forms, regardless of where it exists. Yet while Chomsky has his critics, ranging from notables such as Sheldon Wolin and Martha Nussbaum to a host of less informed interlocutors, he rarely shies away from a reasoned debate, often elevating such exchanges to a new level of understanding and, in some cases, embarrassment for his opponents. Some of his more illustrious and infamous debaters have included Michel Foucault, William Buckley Jr., John Silber, Christopher Hitchens, Alan Dershowitz and Slavoj Žižek. At the same time, he has refused, in spite of the occasional and most hateful and insipid of attacks, to mimic such tactics in responding to his less civil denigrators.[4] Some of Chomsky's detractors have accused him of being too strident, not being theoretical enough, or, more recently, not understanding the true nature of ideology. These criticisms seem empty and baseless and appear irrelevant, considering the encouraging impact Chomsky's work has had on younger generations, including many in the Occupy movement and other international resistance networks.

It is important to note that I am not suggesting that Chomsky is somehow an iconic figure who inhabits an intellectual version of celebrity culture. On the contrary, he deplores such a role and is an enormously humble and self-effacing human being. What I am suggesting is that the models for political leadership and civic responsibility put forth in American society for young people and others to learn from, are largely drawn from the ranks of a criminal, if not egregiously anti-democratic, class of elite financers and the rich. Chomsky offers a crucial, though often unacknowledged, standard for how to be engaged with the world such that issues of commitment and courage are tied to considerations of justice and struggle, not merely to the accumulation of capital, regardless of the social costs.

His decisive influence on a range of fields has not only opened up new modes of inquiry but also gives gravitas to the political impulse that underscores such contributions. The point here is neither to idolize nor to demonize Chomsky—the two modalities that often mark reactions to his work. Rather, the issue is to articulate the ways in which Chomsky as a public intellectual gives meaning to the disposition and characteristics that need to be in place for such critical work: a historical consciousness, civic courage, sacrifice, incisiveness, thoughtfulness, rigor, compassion, political interventions, the willingness to be a moral witness and the ability to listen to others.

As a public intellectual, Chomsky speaks to all people to use their talents and resources to promote public values, defend the common good and connect education to social change. He strongly rejects the notion that educators are merely servants of the state and that students are nothing more than consumers in training. The role of educators and academics as public intellectuals has a long history in Chomsky's work and is inextricably connected to defending the university as a public good and democratic public sphere. Chomsky made this clear in a talk he gave at the Modern Language Association in 2000 when he insisted that:

> Universities face a constant struggle to maintain their integrity, and their fundamental social role in a healthy society, in the face of external pressures. The problems are heightened with the expansion of private power in every domain, in the course of the state-corporate social engineering projects of the past several decades. . . . To defend their integrity

and proper commitments is an honorable and difficult task in itself, but our sights should be set higher
than that. Particularly in the societies that are more
privileged, many choices are available, including
fundamental institutional change, if that is the right
way to proceed, and surely including scholarship
that contributes to, and draws from, the never-end-
ing popular struggles for freedom and justice. [5]

Higher education is under attack not because it is failing,
but because it is a potentially democratic public sphere. As
such, conservatives and neoliberals often see it as a dangerous
institution that reminds them of the rebellious legacy of the
1960s, when universities were the center of struggles over free
speech, anti-racist and feminist pedagogies, and the anti-war
movement. Higher education has become a target for right-
wing ideologues and the corporate elite because it is capable
of teaching students how to think critically, and it offers the
promise of new modes of solidarity to students outside of the
exchange value proffered by neoliberal instrumentalism and
the reduction of education to forms of training.

In a wide-ranging and brilliant essay on higher education in this book, Chomsky not only lays out the reasons why
public education is under attack, but also provides a critical
reading of those historical forces such as the Trilateral Commission and the Powell memorandum of 1971, which made
quite clear that the purpose of education was to "indoctrinate
the young." He then points to the various measures used by
the financial elite and the right wing, extending from defunding the university and imposing a corporate business model
on it to disempowering faculty, destroying unions and elimi-
nating tenure for the vast majority to disciplining students by
burdening them with overwhelming debt. For Chomsky, any

crisis can only be understood if it is situated in its historical genealogy. A lesson too often forgotten in an age in which speed overtakes any attention to public memory and insightful contemplation.

Chomsky extends the democratic legacy of higher education by insisting that universities and faculty should press the claims for economic and social justice. He also argues more specifically that while higher education should be revered for its commitment to disinterested truth and reason, it also has a crucial role to play in its opposition to the permanent warfare state, the war on the poor, the squelching of dissent by the surveillance state, the increasing violence waged against students, and the rise of an authoritarian state engaged in targeted assassination, drone warfare and the destruction of the environment. Part of that role is to create an informed and reflective democratic citizenry engaged in the struggle for social justice and equality. Standing for truth is only one role the university can assume, and it is not enough. It must also fulfill its role of being attentive to the needs of young people by safeguarding their interests while educating them to exercise their capacities to fulfill their social, political, economic and ethical responsibilities to others, to broader publics and to the wider global social order. As Chomsky reminds us, caring about other people is a dangerous idea in America today and signals the ongoing drift of the United States from a struggling democracy to an increasingly consolidated authoritarian state.[6]

Chomsky is not content to focus on the perpetrators of global crime and the new forms of authoritarianism that they are consolidating across the globe; he also focuses on "the unpeople" who are now considered disposable, those who have been written out of the discourse of what he considers a tortured democracy, as a force for collective resistance capable of employing new modes of agency and struggle. Whether he is talking about war, education, militarization or the media, there is always in his work a sense of commitment, civic courage and a call for resistance that is breathtaking and moving. His interventions are always political, and yet he manages to avoid the easy mantle of dogmatism or the kind of humiliating clownish performance we see among some alleged leftist intellectuals. Like C. Wright Mills, he has revived the sociological imagination, connecting the totality and the historically specific, a broader passion for the promise of democracy and a complex rendering of the historical narratives of those who are often marginalized and excluded. There is also a refusal to shield the powerful from moral and political critique. Chomsky has become a signpost for an emerging generation of intellectuals who are not only willing to defend the institutions, public spheres and formative cultures that make democracy possible, but also address those anti-democratic forces working diligently to dismantle the conditions that make an aspiring democracy meaningful.

We live at a time when the growing catastrophes that face Americans and the rest of the globe are increasingly matched by the accumulation of power by the rich and financial elite. Their fear of democracy is now strengthened by the financial, political and corporate elite's intensive efforts to normalize their own power and silence those who hold them accountable. For many, we live in a time of utter despair. But resistance is not only possible, it may be more necessary now than at any other time in America's past, given the current dismantling of civil rights and democratic institutions, and the war on women, labor unions and the poor—all accompanied by the rise of a neoliberal regime that views democracy as an excess, if not dangerous, and an obstacle to implementing its ideological and political goals.

Brimming from each page of this book is what Noam

Chomsky has been telling us for over 50 years: Resistance demands a combination of hope, vision, courage and a willingness to make power accountable, all the while connecting with the desires, aspirations and dreams of those whose suffering is both structurally imposed and thus preventable. He has also reminded us again and again through numerous historical examples that public memory contains the flashpoints for remembering that such struggles are always collective and never merely a matter of individual resistance. Movements bring change, and solidarity is key. As Archon Fung points out, Chomsky's role as a public intellectual makes clear the importance of making power visible, holding authority accountable, and engaging in rigorous critique. His work also suggests that in addition to rigorous criticism, public intellectuals can also help to "shape the democratic character of public policy," work with "popular movements and organizations in their efforts to advance justice and democracy," and while refusing to succumb to reformist practices, "join citizens—and sometimes government—to construct a world that is more just and democratic."[7]

He may be one of the few public intellectuals left of an older generation who offers a rare glimpse into what it means to widen the scope of the meaning of political and intellectual inquiry—an intellectual who rethinks in a critical fashion the educative nature of politics within the changed and totalizing conditions of a neoliberal global assault on all vestiges of democracy. He not only trades in ideas that defy scholastic disciplines and intellectual boundaries, he also makes clear that it is crucial to hold ideas accountable for the practices they legitimate and produce, while at the same time refusing to limit critical ideas to simply modes of critique. In this instance, ideas not only challenge the normalizing discourses and representations of commonsense and the power inequities they legitimate, but also open up the possibilities inherent in a discourse that moves beyond the given and points to new ways of thinking and acting about freedom, civic courage, social responsibility and justice from the standpoint of radical democratic ideals.

BECAUSE WE SAY SO may be one of the most insightful collections of Chomsky's work yet published. Throughout his commentaries, he demonstrates that it is not only democracy and human decency that are at risk, but survival itself. In doing so, Chomsky makes clear that the urgency of the times demands understanding and action, critique and hope. This is a book that should and must be read, given the dire times in which we live. For Chomsky, history is open and the time has come to reclaim the promise of a democracy in which justice, liberty, equality and the common good still matter.

Notes

1 See, for example, Noam Chomsky, "The Responsibility of Intellectuals," *NEW YORK REVIEW OF BOOKS* (February 13, 1967). See also an updated version of this essay in Noam Chomsky, "The Responsibility of Intellectuals, Redux: Using Privilege to Challenge the State," *BOSTON REVIEW* (September 1, 2011).

2 "Chomsky book banned at Guantánamo," *SEATTLE TIMES*, October 13, 2009. http://o.staging.seattletimes.com/nation-world/chomsky-book-banned-at-guantnamo/

3 Stuart Hall and Les Back, "In Conversation: At Home and Not at Home," *CULTURAL STUDIES*, Vol. 23, No. 4, (July 2009), pp. 680–681.

4 Over the course of his career, a number of false claims have been attributed to Chomsky, including the absurd notion published in the *NEW YORK TIMES HIGHER EDUCATION SUPPLEMENT* that he was an apologist for the Pol Pot regime, and on another occasion, the damaging charge that he was anti-Semitic, given his defense of freedom of speech, including that of the French historian Robert Faurisson, an alleged Holocaust denier. Chomsky's long-standing critique of totalitarianism in all its forms seems to have been forgotten in these cases.

5 Noam Chomsky, "Paths Taken, Tasks Ahead," *PROFESSION* (2000), p. 38.

6 See, for instance, Noam Chomsky, "America Hates Its Poor," *OCCUPY: REFLECTIONS ON CLASS WAR, REBELLION AND SOLIDARITY* (Westfield, NJ: Zuccotti Park Press, Second Edition, 2013).

7 Archon Fung, "The Constructive Responsibility of Intellectuals," *BOSTON REVIEW*, (September 9, 2011).

MARCHING OFF THE CLIFF

December 5, 2011

A task of the United Nations Framework Convention on Climate Change, now under way in Durban, South Africa, is to extend earlier policy decisions that were limited in scope and only partially implemented.

These decisions trace back to the U.N. Convention of 1992 and the Kyoto Protocol of 1997, which the U.S. refused to join. The Kyoto Protocol's first commitment period ends in 2012. A fairly general pre-conference mood was captured by a *NEW YORK TIMES* headline: "Urgent Issues but Low Expectations."

As the delegates meet in Durban, a report on newly updated digests of polls by the Council on Foreign Relations and the Program on International Policy Attitudes (PIPA) reveals that "publics around the world and in the United States say their government should give global warming a higher priority and strongly support multilateral action to address it."

Most U.S. citizens agree, though PIPA clarifies that the percentage "has been declining over the last few years, so that American concern is significantly lower than the global average—70 percent as compared to 84 percent."

"Americans do not perceive that there is a scientific consensus on the need for urgent action on climate change. . . . A large majority think that they will be personally affected by climate change eventually, but only a minority thinks that they are being affected now, contrary to views in most other countries. Americans tend to underestimate the level of concern among other Americans."

These attitudes aren't accidental. In 2009 the energy industries, backed by business lobbies, launched major campaigns that cast doubt on the near-unanimous consensus of scientists on the severity of the threat of human-induced global warming.

The consensus is only "near-unanimous" because it doesn't include the many experts who feel that climate-change warnings don't go far enough, and the marginal group that deny the threat's validity altogether.

The standard "he says/she says" coverage of the issue keeps to what is called "balance": the overwhelming majority of scientists on one side, the denialists on the other. The scientists who issue the more dire warnings are largely ignored.

One effect is that scarcely one-third of the U.S. population believes that there is a scientific consensus on the threat of global warming—far less than the global average, and radically inconsistent with the facts.

It's no secret that the U.S. government is lagging on climate issues. "Publics around the world in recent years have largely disapproved of how the United States is handling the problem of climate change," according to PIPA. "In general, the United States has been most widely seen as the country having the most negative effect on the world's environment, followed by China. Germany has received the best ratings."

To gain perspective on what's happening in the world, it's sometimes useful to adopt the stance of intelligent extraterrestrial observers viewing the strange doings on Earth. They would be watching in wonder as the richest and most powerful country in world history now leads the lemmings cheerfully off the cliff.

Last month, the International Energy Agency (IEA), which was formed on the initiative of U.S. Secretary of State Henry Kissinger in 1974, issued its latest report on rapidly increasing carbon emissions from fossil fuel use.

The IEA estimated that if the world continues on its

present course, the "carbon budget" will be exhausted by 2017. The budget is the quantity of emissions that can keep global warming at the 2 degrees Celsius level considered the limit of safety.

IEA chief economist Fatih Birol said, "The door is closing . . . if we don't change direction now on how we use energy, we will end up beyond what scientists tell us is the minimum (for safety). The door will be closed forever."

Also last month, the U.S. Department of Energy reported the emissions figures for 2010. Emissions "jumped by the biggest amount on record," the Associated Press reported, meaning that "levels of greenhouse gases are higher than the worst-case scenario" anticipated by the Intergovernmental Panel on Climate Change (IPCC) in 2007.

John Reilly, co-director of the Massachusetts Institute of Technology's (MIT) program on climate change, told the Associated Press that scientists have generally found the IPCC predictions to be too conservative—unlike the fringe of denialists who gain public attention. Reilly reported that the IPCC's worst-case scenario was about in the middle of the MIT scientists' estimates of likely outcomes.

As these ominous reports were released, the *Financial Times* devoted a full page to the optimistic expectations that the U.S. might become energy-independent for a century with new technology for extracting North American fossil fuels.

Though projections are uncertain, the *Financial Times* reports, the U.S. might "leapfrog Saudi Arabia and Russia to become the world's largest producer of liquid hydrocarbons, counting both crude oil and lighter natural gas liquids."

In this happy event, the U.S. could expect to retain its global hegemony. Beyond some remarks about local ecological impact, the *Financial Times* said nothing about what kind of a world would emerge from these exciting prospects. Energy is to burn; the global environment be damned.

Just about every government is taking at least halting steps to do something about the likely impending catastrophe. The U.S. is leading the way—backward. The Republican-dominated U.S. House of Representatives is now dismantling environmental measures introduced by Richard Nixon, in many respects the last liberal president.

This reactionary behavior is one of many indications of the crisis of U.S. democracy in the past generation. The gap between public opinion and public policy has grown to a chasm on central issues of current policy debate such as the deficit and jobs. However, thanks to the propaganda offensive, the gap is less than what it should be on the most serious issue on the international agenda today—arguably in history.

The hypothetical extraterrestrial observers can be pardoned if they conclude that we seem to be infected by some kind of lethal insanity.

RECOGNIZING THE "UNPEOPLE"

January 5, 2012

On June 15, three months after the NATO bombing of Libya began, the African Union (A.U.) presented to the U.N. Security Council the African position on the attack—in reality, bombing by their traditional imperial aggressors: France and Britain, joined by the United States, which initially coordinated the assault, and marginally some other nations.

It should be recalled that there were two interventions. The first, under U.N. Security Council Resolution 1973, adopted on March 17, 2011, called for a no-fly zone, a cease-fire and measures to protect civilians. After a few moments, that intervention was cast aside as the imperial triumvirate joined the rebel army, serving as its air force.

At the outset of the bombing, the African Union called for efforts at diplomacy and negotiations to try to head off a likely humanitarian catastrophe in Libya. Within the month, the A.U. was joined by the BRICS countries (Brazil, Russia, India, China and South Africa) and others, including the major regional NATO power Turkey.

In fact, the triumvirate was quite isolated in its attacks—undertaken to eliminate the mercurial tyrant whom they had supported when it was advantageous. The hope was for a regime likelier to be amenable to Western demands for control over Libya's rich resources and, perhaps, to offer an African base for the U.S. Africa command (AFRICOM), so far confined to Stuttgart.

No one can know whether the relatively peaceful efforts called for in U.N. Resolution 1973, and backed by most of the world, might have succeeded in averting the terrible loss of life and the destruction that followed in Libya.

On June 15, the African Union informed the Security

Council that "ignoring the A.U. for three months and going on with the bombings of the sacred land of Africa has been high-handed, arrogant and provocative." The African Union went on to present a plan for negotiations and policing within Libya by A.U. forces, along with other measures of reconciliation—to no avail.

The African Union call to the Security Council also laid out the background for their concerns: "Sovereignty has been a tool of emancipation of the peoples of Africa who are beginning to chart transformational paths for most of the African countries after centuries of predation by the slave trade, colonialism and neocolonialism. Careless assaults on the sovereignty of African countries are, therefore, tantamount to inflicting fresh wounds on the destiny of the African peoples."

The African appeal can be found in the Indian journal FRONTLINE, but was mostly unheard in the West. That comes as no surprise: Africans are "unpeople," to adapt George Orwell's term for those unfit to enter history.

On March 12, the Arab League gained the status of people by supporting U.N. Resolution 1973. But approval soon faded when the League withheld support for the subsequent Western bombardment of Libya.

And on April 10, the Arab League reverted to unpeople by calling on the U.N. also to impose a no-fly zone over Gaza and to lift the Israeli siege, virtually ignored.

That too makes good sense. Palestinians are prototypical unpeople, as we see regularly. Consider the November/December issue of FOREIGN AFFAIRS, which opened with two articles on the Israel-Palestine conflict.

One, written by Israeli officials Yosef Kuperwasser and Shalom Lipner, blamed the continuing conflict on the Palestinians for refusing to recognize Israel as a Jewish state (keeping to the diplomatic norm: States are recognized, but not privileged sectors within them).

The second, by American scholar Ronald R. Krebs, attributes the problem to the Israeli occupation; the article is subtitled: "How the Occupation Is Destroying the Nation." Which nation? Israel, of course, harmed by having its boot on the necks of unpeople.

Another illustration: In October, headlines trumpeted the release of Gilad Shalit, the Israeli soldier who had been captured by Hamas. The article in the *New York Times Magazine* was devoted to his family's suffering. Shalit was freed in exchange for hundreds of unpeople, about whom we learned little, apart from sober debate as to whether their release might harm Israel.

We also learned nothing about the hundreds of other detainees held in Israeli prisons for long periods without charge.

Among the unmentioned prisoners are the brothers Osama and Mustafa Abu Muamar, civilians kidnapped by Israeli forces that raided Gaza City on June 24, 2006—the day before Shalit was captured. The brothers were then "disappeared" into Israel's prison system.

Whatever one thinks of capturing a soldier from an attacking army, kidnapping civilians is plainly a far more serious crime—unless, of course, they are mere unpeople.

To be sure, these crimes do not compare with many others, among them the mounting attacks on Israel's Bedouin citizens, who live in southern Israel's Negev.

They are again being expelled under a new program designed to destroy dozens of Bedouin villages to which they had been driven earlier. For benign reasons, of course. The Israeli cabinet explained that ten Jewish settlements would be

founded there "to attract a new population to the Negev"—
that is, to replace unpeople with legitimate people. Who
could object to that?

The strange breed of unpeople can be found everywhere,
including the United States: in the prisons that are an international scandal, the food kitchens, the decaying slums.

But examples are misleading. The world's population as
a whole teeters on the edge of a black hole.

We have daily reminders, even from very small inci-
dents—for instance, last month, when Republicans in the
U.S. House of Representatives barred a virtually costless re-
organization to investigate the causes of the weather extremes
of 2011 and to provide better forecasts.

Republicans feared that it might be an opening wedge
for "propaganda" on global warming, a nonproblem according to the catechism recited by the candidates for the nomina-
tion of what years ago used to be an authentic political party.

Poor sad species.

ANNIVERSARIES FROM "UNHISTORY"

February 4, 2012

George Orwell coined the useful term "unperson" for creatures denied personhood because they don't abide by state doctrine. We may add the term "unhistory" to refer to the fate of unpersons, expunged from history on similar grounds.

The unhistory of unpersons is illuminated by the fate of anniversaries. Important ones are usually commemorated, with due solemnity when appropriate: Pearl Harbor, for example. Some are not, and we can learn a lot about ourselves by extricating them from unhistory.

Right now we are failing to commemorate an event of great human significance: the 50th anniversary of President Kennedy's decision to launch the direct invasion of South Vietnam, soon to become the most extreme crime of aggression since World War II.

Kennedy ordered the U.S. Air Force to bomb South Vietnam (by February 1962, hundreds of missions had flown); authorized chemical warfare to destroy food crops so as to starve the rebellious population into submission; and set in motion the programs that ultimately drove millions of villagers into urban slums and virtual concentration camps, or "Strategic Hamlets." There the villagers would be "protected" from the indigenous guerrillas whom, as the administration knew, they were willingly supporting.

Official efforts at justifying the attacks were slim, and mostly fantasy.

Typical was the president's impassioned address to the American Newspaper Publishers Association on April 27, 1961, where he warned that "we are opposed around the world by a monolithic and ruthless conspiracy that relies primarily on covert means for expanding its sphere of influence."

At the United Nations on September 25, 1961, Kennedy said that if this conspiracy achieved its ends in Laos and Vietnam, "the gates will be opened wide."

The short-term effects were reported by the highly respected Indochina specialist and military historian Bernard Fall—no dove, but one of those who cared about the people of the tormented countries.

In early 1965 he estimated that about 66,000 South Vietnamese had been killed between 1957 and 1961, and another 89,000 between 1961 and April 1965, mostly victims of the U.S. client regime or "the crushing weight of American armor, napalm, jet bombers and finally vomiting gases."

The decisions were kept in the shadows, as are the shocking consequences that persist. To mention just one illustration: SCORCHED EARTH, by Fred Wilcox, the first serious study of the horrifying and continuing impact of chemical warfare on the Vietnamese, appeared a few months ago—and is likely to join other works of unhistory. The core of history is what happened. The core of unhistory is to "disappear" what happened.

By 1967, opposition to the crimes in South Vietnam had reached a substantial scale. Hundreds of thousands of U.S. troops were rampaging through South Vietnam, and heavily populated areas were subjected to intense bombing. The invasion had spread to the rest of Indochina.

The consequences had become so horrendous that Bernard Fall forecast that "Vietnam as a cultural and historic entity . . . is threatened with extinction . . . [as] . . . the countryside literally dies under the blows of the largest military machine ever unleashed on an area of this size."

When the war ended eight devastating years later, mainstream opinion was divided between those who called it a "noble cause" that could have been won with more dedication; and at the opposite extreme, the critics, to whom it was "a mistake" that proved too costly.

Still to come was the bombing of the remote peasant society of northern Laos, executed with such magnitude that victims lived in caves for years to try to survive; and shortly afterward the bombing of rural Cambodia, which surpassed the level of all Allied bombing in the Pacific theater during World War II.

In 1970 U.S. National Security Advisor Henry Kissinger had ordered "a massive bombing campaign in Cambodia. Anything that flies on anything that moves"—a call for genocide of a kind rarely found in the archival record.

Laos and Cambodia were "secret wars," in that reporting was scanty and the facts are still little-known to either the general public or even educated elites, who nonetheless can recite by heart every real or alleged crime of official enemies.

Another chapter in the overflowing annals of unhistory.

In three years we may—or may not—commemorate another event of great contemporary relevance: the 900th anniversary of the Magna Carta.

This document is the foundation for what historian Margaret E. McGuiness, referring to the Nuremberg Trials, hailed as a "particularly American brand of legalism: punishment only for those who could be proved to be guilty through a fair trial with a panoply of procedural protections."

The Great Charter declares that "no free man" shall be deprived of rights "except by the lawful judgment of his peers and by the law of the land." The principles were later broadened to apply to men generally. They crossed the Atlantic and entered into the U.S. Constitution and Bill of Rights, which declared that no "person" can be deprived of rights without due process and a speedy trial.

The founders of course did not intend the term "person" to actually apply to *all* persons. Native Americans were not persons. Neither were those who were enslaved. Women were scarcely persons. However, let us keep to the core notion of presumption of innocence, which has been cast into the oblivion of unhistory.

A further step in undermining the principles of the Magna Carta was taken when President Obama signed the National Defense Authorization Act, which codifies Bush-Obama practice of indefinite detention without trial under military custody.

Such treatment is now mandatory in the case of those accused of aiding enemy forces during the "war on terror," or optional if those accused are American citizens.

The scope is illustrated by the first Guantánamo case to come to trial under President Obama: that of Omar Khadr, a former child soldier accused of the heinous crime of trying to defend his Afghan village when it was attacked by U.S. forces. Captured at age 15, Khadr was imprisoned for eight years in Bagram and Guantánamo, then brought to a military court in October 2010, where he was given the choice of pleading not guilty and staying in Guantánamo forever, or pleading guilty and serving only eight more years. Khadr chose the latter.

Many other examples illuminate the concept of "terrorist." One is Nelson Mandela, only removed from the terrorist list in 2008. Another was Saddam Hussein. In 1982 Iraq was removed from the list of terrorist-supporting states so that the Reagan administration could provide Hussein with aid after he invaded Iran.

Accusation is capricious, without review or recourse, and commonly reflecting policy goals—in Mandela's case, to justify President Reagan's support for the apartheid state's crimes in defending itself against one of the world's "more notorious terrorist groups": Mandela's African National Congress.

All better consigned to unhistory.

WHAT ARE IRAN'S INTENTIONS?

March 1, 2012

The January/February issue of *FOREIGN AFFAIRS* featured the article "Time to Attack Iran: Why a Strike Is the Least Bad Option," by Matthew Kroenig, along with commentary about other ways to contain the Iranian threat.

The media resound with warnings about a likely Israeli attack on Iran while the U.S. hesitates, keeping open the option of aggression—thus again routinely violating the U.N. Charter, the foundation of international law.

As tensions escalate, eerie echoes of the run-up to the wars in Afghanistan and Iraq are in the air. Feverish U.S. primary campaign rhetoric adds to the drumbeat.

Concerns about "the imminent threat" of Iran are often attributed to the "international community"—code language for U.S. allies. The people of the world, however, tend to see matters rather differently.

The Non-Aligned Movement, with 120 member nations, has vigorously supported Iran's right to enrich uranium—an opinion shared by the majority of Americans (as surveyed by WorldPublicOpinion.org) before the massive propaganda onslaught of the past two years.

China and Russia oppose U.S. policy on Iran, as does India, which announced that it would disregard U.S. sanctions and increase trade with Iran. Turkey has followed a similar course.

Europeans regard Israel as the greatest threat to world peace. In the Arab world, Iran is disliked but seen as a threat only by a very small minority. Rather, Israel and the United States are regarded as the pre-eminent threat. A majority think that the region would be more secure if Iran had nuclear weapons: In Egypt on the eve of the Arab Spring,

90 percent held this opinion, according to Brookings Institution/Zogby International polls.

Western commentary has made much of how the Arab dictators allegedly support the U.S. position on Iran, while ignoring the fact that the vast majority of the population opposes it—a stance too revealing to require comment.

Concerns about Israel's nuclear arsenal have long been expressed by some observers in the United States as well. Gen. Lee Butler, former head of the U.S. Strategic Command, described Israel's nuclear weapons as "dangerous in the extreme." In a U.S. Army journal, Lt. Col. Warner Farr wrote that one "purpose of Israeli nuclear weapons, not often stated, but obvious, is their 'use' on the United States"—presumably to ensure consistent U.S. support for Israeli policies.

A prime concern right now is that Israel will seek to provoke some Iranian action that will incite a U.S. attack.

One of Israel's leading strategic analysts, Zeev Maoz, in *DEFENDING THE HOLY LAND*, his comprehensive analysis of Israeli security and foreign policy, concludes that "the balance sheet of Israel's nuclear policy is decidedly negative"—harmful to the state's security. He urges instead that Israel should seek a regional agreement to ban weapons of mass destruction: a WMD-free zone, called for by a 1974 U.N. General Assembly resolution.

Meanwhile, the West's sanctions on Iran are having their usual effect, causing shortages of basic food supplies—not for the ruling clerics but for the population. Small wonder that the sanctions are condemned by Iran's courageous opposition.

The sanctions against Iran may have the same effect as their predecessors against Iraq, which were condemned as "genocidal" by the respected U.N. diplomats who administered them before finally resigning in protest.

The Iraq sanctions devastated the population and

strengthened Saddam Hussein, probably saving him from the fate of a rogues' gallery of other tyrants supported by the U.S.-U.K.—tyrants who prospered virtually to the day when various internal revolts overthrew them.

There is little credible discussion of just what constitutes the Iranian threat, though we do have an authoritative answer, provided by U.S. military and intelligence. Their presentations to Congress make it clear that Iran doesn't pose a military threat.

Iran has very limited capacity to deploy force, and its strategic doctrine is defensive, designed to deter invasion long enough for diplomacy to take effect. If Iran is developing nuclear weapons (which is still undetermined), that would be part of its deterrent strategy.

The understanding of serious Israeli and U.S. analysts is expressed clearly by 30-year CIA veteran Bruce Riedel, who said in January, "If I was an Iranian national security planner, I would want nuclear weapons" as a deterrent.

An additional charge the West levels against Iran is that it is seeking to expand its influence in neighboring countries attacked and occupied by the United States and Britain, and is supporting resistance to the U.S.-backed Israeli aggression in Lebanon and illegal Israeli occupation of Palestinian lands. Like its deterrence of possible violence by Western countries, Iran's actions are said to be intolerable threats to "global order."

Global opinion agrees with Maoz. Support is overwhelming for a WMD-free zone in the Middle East; this zone would include Iran, Israel and preferably the other two nuclear powers that have refused to join the Nuclear Non-Proliferation Treaty: India and Pakistan, who, along with Israel, developed their programs with U.S. aid.

Support for this policy at the NPT Review Conference

in May 2010 was so strong that Washington was forced to agree formally, but with conditions: The zone could not take effect until a comprehensive peace settlement between Israel and its Arab neighbors was in place; Israel's nuclear weapons programs must be exempted from international inspection; and no country (meaning the U.S.) must be obliged to provide information about "Israeli nuclear facilities and activities, including information pertaining to previous nuclear transfers to Israel."

The 2010 conference called for a session in May 2012 to move toward establishing a WMD-free zone in the Middle East.

With all the furor about Iran, however, there is scant attention to that option, which would be the most constructive way of dealing with the nuclear threats in the region: for the "international community," the threat that Iran might gain nuclear capability; for most of the world, the threat posed by the only state in the region with nuclear weapons and a long record of aggression, and its superpower patron.

One can find no mention at all of the fact that the U.S. and Britain have a unique responsibility to dedicate their efforts to this goal. In seeking to provide a thin legal cover for their invasion of Iraq, they invoked U.N. Security Council Resolution 687 (1991), which they claimed Iraq was violating by developing WMD.

We may ignore the claim, but not the fact that the resolution explicitly commits signers to establishing a WMD-free zone in the Middle East.

THE ASSAULT ON PUBLIC EDUCATION

April 3, 2012

Public education is under attack around the world, and in response, student protests have recently been held in Britain, Canada, Chile, Taiwan and elsewhere.

California is also a battleground. The *Los Angeles Times* reports on another chapter in the campaign to destroy what had been the greatest public higher education system in the world: "California State University officials announced plans to freeze enrollment next spring at most campuses and to wait-list all applicants the following fall pending the outcome of a proposed tax initiative on the November ballot."

Similar defunding is under way nationwide. "In most states," the *New York Times* reports, "it is now tuition payments, not state appropriations, that cover most of the budget," so that "the era of affordable four-year public universities, heavily subsidized by the state, may be over."

Community colleges increasingly face similar prospects—and the shortfalls extend to grades K-12.

"There has been a shift from the belief that we as a nation benefit from higher education, to a belief that it's the people receiving the education who primarily benefit and so they should foot the bill," concludes Ronald G. Ehrenberg, a trustee of the State University system of New York and director of the Cornell Higher Education Research Institute.

A more accurate description, I think, is *Failure by Design*, the title of a recent study by the Economic Policy Institute, which has long been a major source of reliable information and analysis on the state of the economy.

The EPI study reviews the consequences of the transformation of the economy a generation ago from domestic production to financialization and offshoring. By design; there have always been alternatives.

One primary justification for the design is what Nobel laureate Joseph Stiglitz called the "religion" that "markets lead to efficient outcomes," which was recently dealt yet another crushing blow by the collapse of the housing bubble that was ignored on doctrinal grounds, triggering the current financial crisis.

Claims are also made about the alleged benefits of the radical expansion of financial institutions since the 1970s. A more convincing description was provided by Martin Wolf, senior economic correspondent for the FINANCIAL TIMES: "An out-of-control financial sector is eating out the modern market economy from inside, just as the larva of the spider wasp eats out the host in which it has been laid."

The EPI study observes that the FAILURE BY DESIGN is class-based. For the designers, it has been a stunning success, as revealed by the astonishing concentration of wealth in the top 1 percent, in fact the top 0.1 percent, while the majority has been reduced to virtual stagnation or decline.

In short, when they have the opportunity, "the Masters of Mankind" pursue their "vile maxim . . . all for ourselves and nothing for other people," as Adam Smith explained long ago.

Mass public education is one of the great achievements of American society. It has had many dimensions. One purpose was to prepare independent farmers for life as wage laborers who would tolerate what they regarded as virtual slavery.

The coercive element did not pass without notice. Ralph Waldo Emerson observed that political leaders call for popular education because they fear that "This country is filling up with thousands and millions of voters, and you must educate them to keep them from our throats." But educated the right way: Limit their perspectives and understanding, discourage free and independent thought, and train them for obedience.

The "vile maxim" and its implementation have regularly called forth resistance, which in turn evokes the same fears among the elite. Forty years ago there was deep concern that the population was breaking free of apathy and obedience.

At the liberal internationalist extreme, the Trilateral Commission—the nongovernmental policy group from which the Carter Administration was largely drawn—issued stern warnings in 1975 that there is too much democracy, in part due to the failures of the institutions responsible for "the indoctrination of the young." On the right, an important 1971 memorandum by Lewis Powell, directed to the U.S. Chamber of Commerce, the main business lobby, wailed that radicals were taking over everything—universities, media, government, etc.—and called on the business community to use its economic power to reverse the attack on our prized way of life—which he knew well. As a lobbyist for the tobacco industry, he was quite familiar with the workings of the nanny state for the rich that he called "the free market."

Since then, many measures have been taken to restore discipline. One is the crusade for privatization—placing control in reliable hands.

Another is sharp increases in tuition, up nearly 600 percent since 1980. These produce a higher education system with "far more economic stratification than is true of any other country," according to Jane Wellman, former director of the Delta Cost Project, which monitors these issues. Tuition increases trap students into long-term debt and hence subordination to private power.

Justifications are offered on economic grounds, but are singularly unconvincing. In countries rich to poor, including Mexico next-door, tuition remains free or nominal. That was true as well in the United States itself when it was a much poorer country after World War II and huge numbers of students were able to enter college under the GI bill—a factor in uniquely high economic growth, even putting aside the significance in improving lives.

Another device is the corporatization of the universities. That has led to a dramatic increase in layers of administration, often professional instead of drawn from the faculty as before; and to imposition of a business culture of "efficiency"—an ideological notion, not just an economic one.

One illustration is the decision of state colleges to eliminate programs in nursing, engineering and computer science, because they are costly—and happen to be the professions where there is a labor shortage, as the *NEW YORK TIMES* reports. The decision harms the society but conforms to the business ideology of short-term gain without regard for human consequences, in accord with the vile maxim.

Some of the most insidious effects are on teaching and monitoring. The Enlightenment ideal of education was captured in the image of education as laying down a string that students follow in their own ways, developing their creativity and independence of mind.

The alternative, to be rejected, is the image of pouring water into a vessel—and a very leaky one, as all of us know from experience. The latter approach includes teaching to test and other mechanisms that destroy students' interest and seek to fit them into a mold, easily controlled. All too familiar today.

CARTEGENA: BEYOND THE SECRET SERVICE SCANDAL

May 1, 2012

Though sidelined by the Secret Service scandal, last month's Summit of the Americas in Cartagena, Colombia, was an event of considerable significance. There are three major reasons: Cuba, the drug war, and the isolation of the United States.

A headline in the *JAMAICA OBSERVER* read, "Summit shows how much Yanqui influence had waned." The story reports that "the big items on the agenda were the lucrative and destructive drug trade and how the countries of the entire region could meet while excluding one country—Cuba."

The meetings ended with no agreement because of U.S. opposition on those items—a drug-decriminalization policy and the Cuba ban. Continued U.S. obstructionism may well lead to the displacement of the Organization of American States by the newly formed Community of Latin American and Caribbean States, from which the United States and Canada are excluded.

Cuba had agreed not to attend the summit because otherwise Washington would have boycotted it. But the meetings made clear that U.S. intransigence would not be long tolerated. The U.S. and Canada were alone in barring Cuban participation, on grounds of Cuba's violations of democratic principles and human rights.

Latin Americans can evaluate these charges from ample experience. They are familiar with the U.S. record on human rights. Cuba especially has suffered from U.S. terrorist attacks and economic strangulation as punishment for its independence—its "successful defiance" of U.S. policies tracing back to the Monroe Doctrine.

Latin Americans don't have to read U.S. scholarship to

recognize that Washington supports democracy if, and only if, it conforms to strategic and economic objectives, and even when it does, favors "limited, top-down forms of democratic change that [do] not risk upsetting the traditional structures of power with which the United States has long been allied . . . [in] quite undemocratic societies," as neo-Reaganite scholar Thomas Carothers points out.

At the Cartagena summit, the drug war became a key issue at the initiative of newly elected Guatemalan President Gen. Pérez Molina, whom no one would mistake for a soft-hearted liberal. He was joined by the summit host, Colombian President Juan Manuel Santos, and by others.

The concern is nothing new. Three years ago the Latin American Commission on Drugs and Democracy published a report on the drug war by ex-Presidents Fernando Henrique Cardoso of Brazil, Ernesto Zedillo of Mexico, and César Gaviria of Colombia calling for decriminalizing marijuana and treating drug use as a public-health problem.

Much research, including a widely quoted Rand Corporation study of 1994, has shown that prevention and treatment are considerably more cost-effective than the coercive measures that receive the bulk of funding. Such nonpunitive measures are also of course far more humane.

Experience conforms to these conclusions. By far the most lethal substance is tobacco, which also kills nonusers at a high rate (passive smoking). Usage has sharply declined among more educated sectors, not by criminalization but as a result of lifestyle changes.

One country, Portugal, decriminalized all drugs in 2001—meaning that they remain technically illegal but are considered administrative violations, removed from the criminal domain. A Cato Institute study by Glenn Greenwald found the results to be "a resounding success. Within this success lie self-evident lessons that should guide drug policy debates around the world."

In dramatic contrast, the coercive procedures of the 40-year U.S. drug war have had virtually no effect on use or price of drugs in the United States, while creating havoc through the continent. The problem is primarily in the United States: both demand (for drugs) and supply (of arms). Latin Americans are the immediate victims, suffering appalling levels of violence and corruption, with addiction spreading through the transit routes.

When policies are pursued for many years with unremitting dedication though they are known to fail in terms of proclaimed objectives, and alternatives that are likely to be far more effective are systematically ignored, questions naturally arise about motives. One rational procedure is to explore predictable consequences. These have never been obscure.

In Colombia, the drug war has been a thin cover for counterinsurgency. Fumigation—a form of chemical warfare—has destroyed crops and rich biodiversity, and contributes to driving millions of poor peasants into urban slums, opening vast territories for mining, agribusiness, ranches and other benefits to the powerful.

Other drug-war beneficiaries are banks laundering massive amounts of money. In Mexico, the major drug cartels are involved in 80 percent of the productive sectors of the economy, according to academic researchers. Similar developments are occurring elsewhere.

In the United States, the primary victims have been African American males, increasingly also women and Hispanics—in short, those rendered superfluous by the economic changes instituted in the 1970s, shifting the economy toward financialization and offshoring of production.

Thanks largely to the highly selective drug war, people

of color are dispatched to prison—the major factor in the radical rise of incarceration since the 1980s that has become an international scandal. The process resembles "social cleansing" in U.S. client states in Latin America, which gets rid of "undesirables."

The isolation of the U.S. at Cartagena carries forward other turning-point developments of the past decade, as Latin America has at last begun to extricate itself from the control of the great powers, and even to address its shocking internal problems.

Latin America has long had a tradition of liberal jurisprudence and rebellion against imposed authority. The New Deal drew from that tradition. Latin Americans may yet again inspire progress in human rights in the United States.

SOMEBODY ELSE'S ATROCITIES

June 1, 2012

In his penetrating study *IDEAL ILLUSIONS: HOW THE U.S. GOVERNMENT CO-OPTED HUMAN RIGHTS*, international affairs scholar James Peck observes, "In the history of human rights, the worst atrocities are always committed by somebody else, never us"—whoever "us" is.

Almost any moment in history yields innumerable illustrations. Let's keep to the past few weeks.

On May 10, the Summer Olympics were inaugurated at the Greek birthplace of the ancient games. A few days before, virtually unnoticed, the government of Vietnam addressed a letter to the International Olympic Committee expressing the "profound concerns of the Government and people of Viet Nam about the decision of IOC to accept the Dow Chemical Company as a global partner sponsoring the Olympic Movement."

Dow provided the chemicals that Washington used from 1961 onward to destroy crops and forests in South Vietnam, drenching the country with Agent Orange.

These poisons contain dioxin, one of the most lethal carcinogens known, affecting millions of Vietnamese and many U.S. soldiers. To this day in Vietnam, aborted fetuses and deformed infants are very likely the effects of these crimes—though, in light of Washington's refusal to investigate, we have only the studies of Vietnamese scientists and independent analysts.

Joining the Vietnamese appeal against Dow are the government of India, the Indian Olympic Association, and the survivors of the horrendous 1984 Bhopal gas leak, one of history's worst industrial disasters, which killed thousands and injured more than half a million.

Union Carbide, the corporation responsible for the disaster, was taken over by Dow, for whom the matter is of no slight concern. In February, Wikileaks revealed that Dow hired the U.S. private investigative agency Stratfor to monitor activists seeking compensation for the victims and prosecution of those responsible.

Another major crime with very serious persisting effects is the Marine assault on the Iraqi city of Fallujah in November 2004.

Women and children were permitted to escape if they could. After several weeks of bombing, the attack opened with a carefully planned war crime: invasion of the Fallujah General Hospital, where patients and staff were ordered to the floor, their hands tied. Soon the bonds were loosened; the compound was secure.

The official justification was that the hospital was reporting civilian casualties, and therefore was considered a propaganda weapon.

Much of the city was left in "smoking ruins," the press reported while the Marines sought out insurgents in their "warrens." The invaders barred entry to the Red Crescent relief organization. Absent an official inquiry, the scale of the crimes is unknown.

If the Fallujah events are reminiscent of the events that took place in the Bosnian enclave of Srebrenica, now again in the news with the genocide trial of Bosnian Serb military commander Ratko Mladic, there's a good reason. An honest comparison would be instructive, but there's no fear of that: One is an atrocity, the other not, by definition.

As in Vietnam, independent investigators are reporting long-term effects of the Fallujah assault.

Medical researchers have found dramatic increases in infant mortality, cancer and leukemia, even higher than Hiroshima and Nagasaki. Uranium levels in hair and soil samples are far beyond comparable cases.

One of the rare investigators from the invading countries is Dr. Kypros Nicolaides, director of the fetal-medicine research center at London's King's College Hospital. "I'm sure the Americans used weapons that caused these deformities," Nicolaides says.

The lingering effects of a vastly greater nonatrocity were reported last month by U.S. law professor James Anaya, the U.N. rapporteur on the rights of indigenous peoples.

Anaya dared to tread on forbidden territory by investigating the shocking conditions among the remnants of the Native American population in the United States—"poverty, poor health conditions, lack of attainment of formal education (and) social ills at rates that far exceed those of other segments of the American population," Anaya reported. No member of Congress was willing to meet him. Press coverage was minimal.

Dissidents have been much in the news after the dramatic rescue of the blind Chinese civil-rights activist Chen Guangcheng.

"The international commotion," Samuel Moyn wrote in the *New York Times* last month, "aroused memories of earlier dissidents like Andrei D. Sakharov and Aleksandr I. Solzhenitsyn, the Eastern bloc heroes of another age who first made 'international human rights' a rallying cry for activists across the globe and a high-profile item on Western governments' agendas."

Moyn is the author of *The Last Utopia: Human Rights in History*, released in 2010. In the *New York Times Book Review*, Belinda Cooper questioned Moyn's tracing the contemporary prominence of these ideals to "(President Jimmy) Carter's abortive steps to inject human rights into foreign policy and the 1975 Helsinki accords with the Soviet Union," focusing on abuses in the Soviet sphere. She finds Moyn's thesis unpersuasive because "an alternative history to his own is far too easy to construct."

True enough: The obvious alternative is the one that James Peck provides, which the mainstream can hardly consider, though the relevant facts are strikingly clear and known at least to scholarship.

Thus in the *CAMBRIDGE HISTORY OF THE COLD WAR*, John Coatsworth recalls that from 1960 to "the Soviet collapse in 1990, the numbers of political prisoners, torture victims, and executions of nonviolent political dissenters in Latin America vastly exceeded those in the Soviet Union and its East European satellites." But being nonatrocities, these crimes, substantially traceable to U.S. intervention, didn't inspire a human-rights crusade.

Also inspired by the Chen rescue, *NEW YORK TIMES* columnist Bill Keller writes that "dissidents are heroic," but they can be "irritants to American diplomats who have important business to transact with countries that don't share our values." Keller criticizes Washington for sometimes failing to live up to our values with prompt action when others commit crimes.

There is no shortage of heroic dissidents within the domains of U.S. influence and power, but they are as invisible as the Latin American victims. Looking almost at random around the world, we find Abdulhadi al-Khawaja, co-founder of the Bahrain Center for Human Rights, an Amnesty International prisoner of conscience, now facing death in prison from a long hunger strike.

And Father Mun Jeong-hyeon, the elderly Korean priest who was severely injured while holding mass as part of the protest against the construction of a U.S. naval base on Jeju

Island, named an Island of Peace, now occupied by security forces for the first time since the 1948 massacres by the U.S.-imposed South Korean government.

And Turkish scholar Ismail Beşikçi, facing trial again for defending the rights of Kurds. He already has spent much of his life in prison on the same charge, including the 1990s, when the Clinton administration was providing Turkey with huge quantities of military aid—at a time when the Turkish military perpetrated some of the period's worst atrocities.

But these instances are all nonexistent, on standard principles, along with others too numerous to mention.

THE GREAT CHARTER:
ITS FATE, OUR FATE

July 3, 2012

THIS TEXT IS ADAPTED FROM AN ADDRESS BY NOAM CHOMSKY ON JUNE 19, 2012, AT THE UNIVERSITY OF ST. ANDREWS IN FIFE, SCOTLAND, AS PART OF ITS 600TH ANNIVERSARY CELEBRATION.

Recent events trace a threatening trajectory, sufficiently so that it may be worthwhile to look ahead a few generations to the millennium anniversary of one of the great events in the establishment of civil and human rights: the issuance of the Magna Carta, the charter of English liberties imposed on King John in 1215.

What we do right now, or fail to do, will determine what kind of world will greet that anniversary. It is not an attractive prospect—not least because the Great Charter is being shredded before our eyes.

The first scholarly edition of the Magna Carta was published in 1759 by the English jurist William Blackstone, whose work was a source for U.S. constitutional law. It was entitled "The Great Charter and the Charter of the Forest," following earlier practice. Both charters are highly significant today.

The first, the Charter of Liberties, is widely recognized to be the cornerstone of the fundamental rights of the English-speaking peoples—or as Winston Churchill put it more expansively, "the charter of every self-respecting man at any time in any land."

In 1679 the Charter was enriched by the Habeas Corpus Act, formally titled "an Act for the better securing the liberty of the subject, and for prevention of imprisonment beyond the seas." The modern harsher version is called "rendition"—imprisonment for the purpose of torture.

Along with much of English law, the Act was incorporated into the U.S. Constitution, which affirms that "the writ of habeas corpus shall not be suspended" except in case of rebellion or invasion. In 1961, the U.S. Supreme Court held that the rights guaranteed by this Act were "(c)onsidered by the Founders as the highest safeguard of liberty."

More specifically, the Constitution provides that no "person [shall] be deprived of life, liberty or property, without due process of law [and] a speedy and public trial" by peers.

The Department of Justice has recently explained that these guarantees are satisfied by internal deliberations in the executive branch, as Jo Becker and Scott Shane reported in the *NEW YORK TIMES* on May 29. Barack Obama, the constitutional lawyer in the White House, agreed. King John would have nodded with satisfaction.

The underlying principle of "presumption of innocence" has also been given an original interpretation. In the calculus of the president's "kill list" of terrorists, "all military-age males in a strike zone" are in effect counted as combatants "unless there is explicit intelligence posthumously proving them innocent," Becker and Shane summarized. Thus post-assassination determination of innocence now suffices to maintain the sacred principle.

This is the merest sample of the dismantling of "the charter of every self-respecting man."

The companion Charter of the Forest is perhaps even more pertinent today. It demanded protection of the commons from external power. The commons were the source of sustenance for the general population—their fuel, their food, their construction materials. The Forest was no wilderness. It was carefully nurtured, maintained in common, its riches available to all, and preserved for future generations.

By the 17th century, the Charter of the Forest had fallen victim to the commodity economy and capitalist practice and morality. No longer protected for cooperative care and use, the commons were restricted to what could not be privatized—a category that continues to shrink before our eyes.

Last month the World Bank ruled that the mining multinational Pacific Rim can proceed with its case against El Salvador for trying to preserve lands and communities from highly destructive gold mining. Environmental protection would deprive the company of future profits, a crime under the rules of the investor rights regime mislabeled as "free trade."

This is only one example of struggles under way over much of the world, some with extreme violence, as in resource-rich eastern Congo, where millions have been killed in recent years to ensure an ample supply of minerals for cellphones and other uses, and of course ample profits.

The dismantling of the Charter of the Forest brought with it a radical revision of how the commons are conceived, captured by Garrett Hardin's influential thesis in 1968 that "Freedom in a commons brings ruin to us all," the famous "tragedy of the commons": What is not privately owned will be destroyed by individual avarice.

The doctrine is not without challenge. Elinor Olstrom won the Nobel Memorial Prize in Economic Sciences in 2009 for her work showing the superiority of user-managed commons.

But the doctrine has force if we accept its unstated premise: that humans are blindly driven by what American workers, at the dawn of the industrial revolution, called "the New Spirit of the Age, Gain Wealth forgetting all but Self"—a doctrine they bitterly condemned as demeaning and destructive, an assault on the very nature of free people.

Huge efforts have been devoted since to inculcating

the New Spirit of the Age. Major industries are dedicated to what political economist Thorstein Veblen called "fabricating wants"—directing people to "the superficial things" of life, like "fashionable consumption," in the words of Columbia University marketing professor Paul Nystrom.

That way people can be atomized, seeking personal gain alone and diverted from dangerous efforts to think for themselves, act in concert and challenge authority.

It's unnecessary to dwell on the extreme dangers posed by one central element of the destruction of the commons: the reliance on fossil fuels, which courts global disaster. Details may be debated, but there is little serious doubt that the problems are all too real and that the longer we delay in addressing them, the more awful will be the legacy left to generations to come. The recent Rio+20 Conference is the latest effort. Its aspirations were meager, its outcome derisory.

In the lead in confronting the crisis, throughout the world, are indigenous communities. The strongest stand has been taken by the one country they govern, Bolivia, the poorest country in South America and for centuries a victim of Western destruction of its rich resources.

After the ignominious collapse of the Copenhagen global climate change summit in 2009, Bolivia organized a People's Summit with 35,000 participants from 140 countries. The summit called for very sharp reduction in emissions, and a Universal Declaration on the Rights of Mother Earth. That is a key demand of indigenous communities all over the world.

The demand is ridiculed by sophisticated Westerners, but unless we can acquire some of the sensibility of the indigenous communities, they are likely to have the last laugh—a laugh of grim despair.

IN HIROSHIMA'S SHADOW

August 1, 2012

August 6, the anniversary of Hiroshima, should be a day of somber reflection, not only on the terrible events of that day in 1945, but also on what they revealed: that humans, in their dedicated quest to extend their capacities for destruction, had finally found a way to approach the ultimate limit.

This year's August 6 memorials have special significance. They take place shortly before the 50th anniversary of "the most dangerous moment in human history," in the words of the historian and John F. Kennedy adviser Arthur M. Schlesinger Jr., referring to the Cuban missile crisis.

Graham Allison writes in the current issue of *FOREIGN AFFAIRS* that Kennedy "ordered actions that he knew would increase the risk not only of conventional war but also nuclear war," with a likelihood of perhaps 50 percent, he believed, an estimate that Allison regards as realistic.

Kennedy declared a high-level nuclear alert that authorized "NATO aircraft with Turkish pilots . . . [or others] . . . to take off, fly to Moscow, and drop a bomb."

None were more shocked by the discovery of missiles in Cuba than the men in charge of the similar missiles that the United States had secretly deployed in Okinawa six months earlier, surely aimed at China, at a moment of elevated regional tensions.

Kennedy took Chairman Nikita Khrushchev "right to the brink of nuclear war and he looked over the edge and had no stomach for it," according to Gen. David Burchinal, then a high-ranking official in the Pentagon planning staff. One can hardly count on such sanity forever.

Khrushchev accepted a formula that Kennedy devised, ending the crisis just short of war. The formula's boldest element, Allison writes, was "a secret sweetener that promised the withdrawal of U.S. missiles from Turkey within six months after the crisis was resolved." These were obsolete missiles that were being replaced by far more lethal, and invulnerable, Polaris submarines.

In brief, even at high risk of war of unimaginable destruction, it was felt necessary to reinforce the principle that the United States has the unilateral right to deploy nuclear missiles anywhere, some aimed at China or at the borders of Russia, which had previously placed no missiles outside the USSR. Justifications of course have been offered, but I do not think they withstand analysis.

An accompanying principle is that Cuba had no right to have missiles for defense against what appeared to be an imminent U.S. invasion. The plans for Kennedy's terrorist programs, Operation Mongoose, called for "open revolt and overthrow of the Communist regime" in October 1962, the month of the missile crisis, recognizing that "final success will require decisive U.S. military intervention."

The terrorist operations against Cuba are commonly dismissed by U.S. commentators as insignificant CIA shenanigans. The victims, not surprisingly, see matters rather differently. We can at last hear their voices in Keith Bolender's *VOICES FROM THE OTHER SIDE: AN ORAL HISTORY OF TERRORISM AGAINST CUBA.*

The events of October 1962 are widely hailed as Kennedy's finest hour. Allison offers them as "a guide for how to defuse conflicts, manage great-power relationships, and make sound decisions about foreign policy in general." In particular, today's conflicts with Iran and China.

Disaster was perilously close in 1962, and there has been no shortage of dangerous moments since. In 1973, in the last days of the Arab-Israeli war, Henry Kissinger called a high-level nuclear alert. India and Pakistan have come close to nuclear war. There have been innumerable cases when human intervention aborted nuclear attack only moments before launch after false reports by automated systems. There is much to think about on August 6.

Allison joins many others in regarding Iran's nuclear programs as the most severe current crisis, "an even more complex challenge for American policymakers than the Cuban missile crisis" because of the threat of Israeli bombing.

The war against Iran is already well under way, including assassination of scientists and economic pressures that have reached the level of "undeclared war," in the judgment of the Iran specialist Gary Sick.

Great pride is taken in the sophisticated cyberwar directed against Iran. The Pentagon regards cyberwar as "an act of war" that authorizes the target "to respond using traditional military force," the *WALL STREET JOURNAL* reports. With the usual exception: not when the United States or an ally is the perpetrator.

The Iran threat has recently been outlined by Gen. Giora Eiland, one of Israel's top military planners, described as "one of the most ingenious and prolific thinkers the [Israeli military] has ever produced."

Of the threats he outlines, the most credible is that "any confrontation on our borders will take place under an Iranian nuclear umbrella." Israel might therefore be constrained in resorting to force. Eiland agrees with the Pentagon and U.S. intelligence, which also regard deterrence as the major threat that Iran poses.

The current escalation of the "undeclared war" against Iran increases the threat of accidental large-scale war. Some of the dangers were illustrated last month when a U.S. naval vessel, part of the huge deployment in the Gulf, fired on a small fishing boat, killing one Indian crew member and wounding at least three others. It would not take much to set off a major war.

One sensible way to avoid such dread consequences is to pursue "the goal of establishing in the Middle East a zone free from weapons of mass destruction and all missiles for their delivery and the objective of a global ban on chemical weapons"—the wording of Security Council resolution 687 of April 1991, which the U.S. and U.K. invoked in their effort to provide a thin legal cover for their invasion of Iraq 12 years later.

The goal has been an Arab-Iranian objective since 1974, regularly re-endorsed, and by now it has near-unanimous global support, at least formally. An international conference to consider ways to implement such a treaty may take place in December.

Progress is unlikely unless there is mass public support in the West. Failure to grasp the opportunity will, once again, lengthen the grim shadow that has darkened the world since that fateful August 6.

WHEN TRAVESTY BORDERS ON TRAGEDY
August 30, 2012

It is not easy to escape from one's skin, to see the world differently from the way it is presented to us day after day. But it is useful to try. Let's take a few examples.

The war drums are beating ever more loudly over Iran. Imagine the situation to be reversed.

Iran is carrying out a murderous and destructive low-level war against Israel with great-power participation. Its leaders announce that negotiations are going nowhere. Israel refuses to sign the Non-Proliferation Treaty and allow inspections, as Iran has done. Israel continues to defy the overwhelming international call for a nuclear-weapons-free zone in the region. Throughout, Iran enjoys the support of its superpower patron.

Iranian leaders are therefore announcing their intention to bomb Israel, and prominent Iranian military analysts report that the attack may happen before the U.S. elections.

Iran can use its powerful air force and new submarines sent by Germany, armed with nuclear missiles and stationed off the coast of Israel. Whatever the timetable, Iran is counting on its superpower backer to join if not lead the assault. U.S. defense secretary Leon Panetta says that while we do not favor such an attack, as a sovereign country Iran will act in its best interests.

All unimaginable, of course, though it is actually happening, with the cast of characters reversed. True, analogies are never exact, and this one is unfair—to Iran.

Like its patron, Israel resorts to violence at will. It persists in illegal settlement in occupied territory, some annexed, all in brazen defiance of international law and the U.N. Security Council. It has repeatedly carried out brutal attacks against Lebanon and the imprisoned people of Gaza, killing tens of thousands without credible pretext.

Thirty years ago Israel destroyed an Iraqi nuclear reactor, an act that has recently been praised, avoiding the strong evidence, even from U.S. intelligence, that the bombing did not end Saddam Hussein's nuclear weapons program but rather initiated it. Bombing of Iran might have the same effect.

Iran too has carried out aggression—but during the past several hundred years, only under the U.S.-backed regime of the shah, when it conquered Arab islands in the Persian Gulf.

Iran engaged in nuclear development programs under the shah, with the strong support of official Washington. The Iranian government is brutal and repressive, as are Washington's allies in the region. The most important ally, Saudi Arabia, is the most extreme Islamic fundamentalist regime, and spends enormous funds spreading its radical Wahhabist doctrines elsewhere. The gulf dictatorships, also favored U.S. allies, have harshly repressed any popular effort to join the Arab Spring.

The Non-Aligned Movement—the governments of most of the world's population—is now meeting in Teheran. The group has vigorously endorsed Iran's right to enrich uranium, and some members—India, for example—adhere to the harsh U.S. sanctions program only partially and reluctantly.

The NAM delegates doubtless recognize the threat that dominates discussion in the West, lucidly articulated by Gen. Lee Butler, former head of the U.S. Strategic Command: "It is dangerous in the extreme that in the cauldron of animosities that we call the Middle East," one nation should arm itself with nuclear weapons, which "inspires other nations to do so."

Butler is not referring to Iran, but to Israel, which is regarded in the Arab countries and in Europe as posing the greatest threat to peace. In the Arab world, the United States is ranked second as a threat, while Iran, though disliked, is far less feared. Indeed in many polls majorities hold that the region would be more secure if Iran had nuclear weapons to balance the threats they perceive.

If Iran is indeed moving toward nuclear-weapons capability—this is still unknown to U.S. intelligence—that may be because it is "inspired to do so" by the U.S.-Israeli threats, regularly issued in explicit violation of the U.N. Charter.

Why then is Iran the greatest threat to world peace, as seen in official Western discourse? The primary reason is acknowledged by U.S. military and intelligence and their Israeli counterparts: Iran might deter the resort to force by the United States and Israel.

Furthermore, Iran must be punished for its "successful defiance," which was Washington's charge against Cuba half a century ago, and still the driving force for the U.S. assault against Cuba that continues despite international condemnation.

Other events featured on the front pages might also benefit from a different perspective. Suppose that Julian Assange had leaked Russian documents revealing important information that Moscow wanted to conceal from the public, and that circumstances were otherwise identical.

Sweden would not hesitate to pursue its sole announced concern, accepting the offer to interrogate Assange in London. It would declare that if Assange returned to Sweden (as he has agreed to do), he would not be extradited to Russia, where chances of a fair trial would be slight.

Sweden would be honored for this principled stand. Assange would be praised for performing a public service—which, of course, would not obviate the need to take the accusations against him as seriously as in all such cases.

The most prominent news story of the day here is the U.S. election. An appropriate perspective was provided by former U.S. Supreme Court Justice Louis Brandeis, who held that "We may have democracy in this country, or we may have wealth concentrated in the hands of a few, but we cannot have both."

Guided by that insight, coverage of the election should focus on the impact of wealth on policy, extensively analyzed in the recent study *AFFLUENCE AND INFLUENCE: ECONOMIC INEQUALITY AND POLITICAL POWER IN AMERICA* by Martin Gilens. He found that the vast majority are "powerless to shape government policy" when their preferences diverge from those of the affluent, who pretty much get what they want when it matters to them.

Small wonder, then, that in a recent ranking of the 31 members of the Organization for Economic Cooperation and Development in terms of social justice, the United States placed 27th, despite its extraordinary advantages.

Or that rational treatment of issues tends to evaporate in the electoral campaign, in ways sometimes verging on comedy.

To take one case, Paul Krugman reports that the much-admired Big Thinker of the Republican Party, Paul Ryan, declares that he derives his ideas about the financial system from a character in a fantasy novel—*ATLAS SHRUGGED*—who calls for the use of gold coins instead of paper currency.

It only remains to draw from a really distinguished writer, Jonathan Swift. In *GULLIVER'S TRAVELS*, his sages of Lagado carry all their goods with them in packs on their backs, and thus could use them for barter without the encumbrance of gold. Then the economy and democracy could truly flourish—and best of all, inequality would sharply decline, a gift to the spirit of Justice Brandeis.

ISSUES THAT OBAMA AND ROMNEY AVOID

October 4, 2012

With the quadrennial presidential election extravaganza reaching its peak, it's useful to ask how the political campaigns are dealing with the most crucial issues we face. The simple answer is: badly, or not at all. If so, some important questions arise: why, and what can we do about it?

There are two issues of overwhelming significance, because the fate of the species is at stake: environmental disaster and nuclear war.

The former is regularly on the front pages. On September 19, for example, Justin Gillis reported in the *New York Times* that the melting of Arctic sea ice had ended for the year, "but not before demolishing the previous record—and setting off new warnings about the rapid pace of change in the region."

The melting is much faster than predicted by sophisticated computer models and the most recent U.N. report on global warming. New data indicate that summer ice might be gone by 2020, with severe consequences. Previous estimates had summer ice disappearing by 2050.

"But governments have not responded to the change with any greater urgency about limiting greenhouse emissions," Gillis writes. "To the contrary, their main response has been to plan for exploitation of newly accessible minerals in the Arctic, including drilling for more oil"—that is, to accelerate the catastrophe.

This reaction demonstrates an extraordinary willingness to sacrifice the lives of our children and grandchildren for short-term gain. Or, perhaps, an equally remarkable willingness to shut our eyes so as not to see the impending peril.

That's hardly all. A new study from the Climate Vulnerability Monitor has found that "climate change caused by global warming is slowing down world economic output by 1.6 percent a year and will lead to a doubling of costs in the next two decades." The study was widely reported elsewhere, but Americans have been spared the disturbing news.

The official Democratic and Republican platforms on climate matters are reviewed in *SCIENCE* magazine's September 14 issue. In a rare instance of bipartisanship, both parties demand that we make the problem worse.

In 2008, both party platforms had devoted some attention to how the government should address climate change. Today, the issue has almost disappeared from the Republican platform—which does, however, demand that Congress "take quick action" to prevent the Environmental Protection Agency, established by former Republican President Richard Nixon in saner days, from regulating greenhouse gases. And we must open Alaska's Arctic refuge to drilling to take "advantage of all our American God-given resources." We cannot disobey the Lord, after all.

The platform also states that "we must restore scientific integrity to our public research institutions and remove political incentives from publicly funded research"—code words for climate science.

The Republican candidate Mitt Romney, seeking to escape from the stigma of what he understood a few years ago about climate change, has declared that there is no scientific consensus, so we should support more debate and investigation—but not action, except to make the problems more serious.

The Democrats mention in their platform that there is a problem, and recommend that we should work "toward an agreement to set emissions limits in unison with other emerging powers." But that's about it.

President Barack Obama has emphasized that we must gain 100 years of energy independence by exploiting fracking and other new technologies—without asking what the world would look like after a century of such practices.

So there are differences between the parties: about how enthusiastically the lemmings should march toward the cliff.

The second major issue, nuclear war, is also on the front pages every day, but in a way that would astound a Martian observing the strange doings on Earth.

The current threat is again in the Middle East, specifically Iran—at least according to the West, that is. In the Middle East, the U.S. and Israel are considered much greater threats.

Unlike Iran, Israel refuses to allow inspections or to sign the Nuclear Non-Proliferation Treaty (NPT). It has hundreds of nuclear weapons and advanced delivery systems, and a long record of violence, aggression and lawlessness, thanks to unremitting American support. Whether Iran is seeking to develop nuclear weapons, U.S. intelligence doesn't know.

In its latest report, the International Atomic Energy Agency says that it cannot demonstrate "the absence of undeclared nuclear material and activities in Iran"—a roundabout way of condemning Iran, as the U.S. demands, while conceding that the agency can add nothing to the conclusions of U.S. intelligence.

Therefore Iran must be denied the right to enrich uranium that is guaranteed by the Nuclear Non-Proliferation Treaty, and endorsed by most of the world, including the nonaligned countries that have just met in Tehran.

The possibility that Iran might develop nuclear weapons arises in the electoral campaign. (The fact that Israel already has them does not.) Two positions are counterposed: Should the U.S. declare that it will attack if Iran reaches the capability to develop nuclear weapons, which dozens of countries enjoy? Or should Washington keep the "red line" more indefinite?

The latter position is that of the White House; the former is demanded by Israeli hawks—and accepted by the U.S. Congress. The Senate just voted 90–1 to support the Israeli position.

Missing from the debate is the obvious way to mitigate or end whatever threat Iran might be believed to pose: Establish a nuclear weapons–free zone in the region. The opportunity is readily available: An international conference is to convene in a few months to pursue this objective, supported by almost the entire world, including a majority of Israelis.

The government of Israel, however, has announced that it will not participate until there is a general peace agreement in the region, which is unattainable as long as Israel persists in its illegal activities in the occupied Palestinian territories. Washington keeps to the same position, and insists that Israel must be excluded from any such regional agreement.

We could be moving toward a devastating war, possibly even nuclear. Straightforward ways exist to overcome this threat, but they will not be taken unless there is large-scale public activism demanding that the opportunity be pursued. This in turn is highly unlikely as long as these matters remain off the agenda, not just in the electoral circus, but in the media and larger national debate.

Elections are run by the public relations industry. Its primary task is commercial advertising, which is designed to undermine markets by creating uninformed consumers who will make irrational choices—the exact opposite of how markets are supposed to work, but certainly familiar to anyone who has watched television.

It's only natural that when enlisted to run elections, the industry would adopt the same procedures in the interests of the paymasters, who certainly don't want to see informed citizens making rational choices.

The victims, however, do not have to obey, in either case. Passivity may be the easy course, but it is hardly the honorable one.

GAZA, THE WORLD'S LARGEST OPEN-AIR PRISON

November 7, 2012

Even a single night in jail is enough to give a taste of what it means to be under the total control of some external force.

And it hardly takes more than a day in Gaza to appreciate what it must be like to try to survive in the world's largest open-air prison, where some 1.5 million people on a roughly 140-square-mile strip of land are subject to random terror and arbitrary punishment, with no purpose other than to humiliate and degrade.

Such cruelty is to ensure that Palestinian hopes for a decent future will be crushed, and that the overwhelming global support for a diplomatic settlement granting basic human rights will be nullified. The Israeli political leadership has dramatically illustrated this commitment in the past few days, warning that they will "go crazy" if Palestinian rights are given even limited recognition by the U.N.

This threat to "go crazy" ("nishtagea")—that is, launch a tough response—is deeply rooted, stretching back to the Labor governments of the 1950s, along with the related "Samson Complex": If crossed, we will bring down the Temple walls around us.

Thirty years ago, Israeli political leaders, including some noted hawks, submitted to Prime Minister Menachem Begin a shocking report on how settlers on the West Bank regularly committed "terrorist acts" against Arabs there, with total impunity.

Disgusted, the prominent military-political analyst Yoram Peri wrote that the Israeli army's task, it seemed, was not to defend the state, but "to demolish the rights of innocent people just because they are Araboushim [a harsh racial epithet] living in territories that God promised to us."

Gazans have been singled out for particularly cruel punishment. Thirty years ago, in his memoir *THE THIRD WAY*, Raja Shehadeh, a lawyer, described the hopeless task of trying to protect fundamental human rights within a legal system designed to ensure failure, and his personal experience as a Samid, "a steadfast one," who watched his home turned into a prison by brutal occupiers and could do nothing but somehow "endure."

Since then, the situation has become much worse. The Oslo Accords, celebrated with much pomp in 1993, determined that Gaza and the West Bank are a single territorial entity. By that time, the United States and Israel had already initiated their program to separate Gaza and the West Bank, so as to block a diplomatic settlement and punish the Araboushim in both territories.

Punishment of Gazans became still more severe in January 2006, when they committed a major crime: They voted the "wrong way" in the first free election in the Arab world, electing Hamas.

Displaying their "yearning for democracy," the United States and Israel, backed by the timid European Union, immediately imposed a brutal siege, along with military attacks. The United States turned at once to its standard operating procedure when a disobedient population elects the wrong government: Prepare a military coup to restore order.

Gazans committed a still greater crime a year later by blocking the coup attempt, leading to a sharp escalation of the siege and attacks. These culminated in winter 2008–2009, with Operation Cast Lead, one of the most cowardly and vicious exercises of military force in recent memory: A defenseless civilian population, trapped, was subjected to relentless attack by one of the world's most advanced military systems, reliant on U.S. arms and protected by U.S. diplomacy.

Of course, there were pretexts—there always are. The usual one, trotted out when needed, is "security": in this case, against homemade rockets from Gaza.

In 2008, a truce was established between Israel and Hamas. Not a single Hamas rocket was fired until Israel broke the truce under cover of the U.S. election on November 4, invading Gaza for no good reason and killing half a dozen Hamas members.

The Israeli government was advised by its highest intelligence officials that the truce could be renewed by easing the criminal blockade and ending military attacks. But the government of Ehud Olmert—himself reputedly a dove—rejected these options, resorting to its huge advantage in violence: Operation Cast Lead.

The internationally respected Gazan human-rights advocate Raji Sourani analyzed the pattern of attack under Cast Lead. The bombing was concentrated in the north, targeting defenseless civilians in the most densely populated areas, with no possible military basis. The goal, Sourani suggests, may have been to drive the intimidated population to the south, near the Egyptian border. But the Samidin—those who resist by enduring—stayed put.

A further goal might have been to drive them beyond the border. From the earliest days of the Zionist colonization it was argued that Arabs have no real reason to be in Palestine: They can be just as happy somewhere else, and should leave—politely "transferred," the doves suggested.

This is surely no small concern in Egypt, and perhaps a reason why Egypt doesn't open the border freely to civilians or even to desperately needed supplies.

Sourani and other knowledgeable sources have observed

that the discipline of the Samidin conceals a powder keg that might explode at any time, unexpectedly, like the first Intifada in Gaza in 1987, after years of repression.

A necessarily superficial impression after spending several days in Gaza is amazement, not only at Gazans' ability to go on with life but also at the vibrancy and vitality among young people, particularly at the university, where I attended an international conference.

But one can detect signs that the pressure may become too hard to bear. Reports indicate that there is simmering frustration among young people—a recognition that under the U.S.-Israeli occupation the future holds nothing for them.

Gaza has the look of a Third World country, with pockets of wealth surrounded by hideous poverty. It is not, however, undeveloped. Rather it is "de-developed," and very systematically so, to borrow the term from Sara Roy, the leading academic specialist on Gaza.

The Gaza Strip could have become a prosperous Mediterranean region, with rich agriculture and a flourishing fishing industry, marvelous beaches and, as discovered a decade ago, good prospects for extensive natural gas supplies within its territorial waters. By coincidence or not, that's when Israel intensified its naval blockade. The favorable prospects were aborted in 1948, when the Strip had to absorb a flood of Palestinian refugees who fled in terror or were forcefully expelled from what became Israel—in some cases months after the formal cease-fire. Israel's 1967 conquests and their aftermath administered further blows, with terrible crimes continuing to the present day.

The signs are easy to see, even on a brief visit. Sitting in a hotel near the shore, one can hear the machine-gun fire of Israeli gunboats driving fishermen out of Gaza's territorial waters and toward land, forcing them to fish in waters that are heavily polluted because of U.S.-Israeli refusal to allow reconstruction of the sewage and power systems they destroyed.

The Oslo Accords laid plans for two desalination plants, a necessity in this arid region. One, an advanced facility, was built: in Israel. The second one is in Khan Yunis, in the south of Gaza. The engineer in charge at Khan Yunis explained that this plant was designed so that it can't use seawater, but must rely on underground water, a cheaper process that further degrades the meager aquifer, guaranteeing severe problems in the future.

The water supply is still severely limited. The U.N. Relief and Works Agency (UNRWA), which cares for refugees but not other Gazans, recently released a report warning that damage to the aquifer may soon become "irreversible," and that without quick remedial action, Gaza may cease to be a "livable place" by 2020.

Israel permits concrete to enter for UNRWA projects, but not for Gazans engaged in the huge reconstruction efforts. The limited heavy equipment mostly lies idle, since Israel does not permit materials for repair.

All this is part of the general program that Dov Weisglass, an adviser to Prime Minister Olmert, described after Palestinians failed to follow orders in the 2006 elections: "The idea," he said, "is to put the Palestinians on a diet, but not to make them die of hunger."

Recently, after several years of effort, the Israeli human rights organization Gisha succeeded in obtaining a court order for the government to release its records detailing plans for the "diet." Jonathan Cook, a journalist based in Israel, summarizes them: "Health officials provided calculations of the minimum number of calories needed by Gaza's 1.5 million inhabitants to avoid malnutrition. Those figures were then translated into truckloads of food Israel was supposed to allow in each day

. . . an average of only 67 trucks—much less than half of the minimum requirement—entered Gaza daily. This compared to more than 400 trucks before the blockade began."

The result of imposing the diet, Middle East scholar Juan Cole observes, is that "about 10 percent of Palestinian children in Gaza under age 5 have had their growth stunted by malnutrition. . . . In addition, anemia is widespread, affecting over two-thirds of infants, 58.6 percent of schoolchildren, and over a third of pregnant mothers."

Raji Sourani, the human-rights advocate, observes that "what has to be kept in mind is that the occupation and the absolute closure is an ongoing attack on the human dignity of the people in Gaza in particular and all Palestinians generally. It is systematic degradation, humiliation, isolation and fragmentation of the Palestinian people."

This conclusion has been confirmed by many other sources. In the *LANCET*, a leading medical journal, Rajaie Batniji, a visiting Stanford physician, describes Gaza as "something of a laboratory for observing an absence of dignity," a condition that has "devastating" effects on physical, mental and social well-being.

"The constant surveillance from the sky, collective punishment through blockade and isolation, the intrusion into homes and communications, and restrictions on those trying to travel, or marry, or work make it difficult to live a dignified life in Gaza," Batniji writes. The Araboushim must be taught not to raise their heads.

There were hopes that Mohammed Morsi's new government in Egypt, which is less in thrall to Israel than the western-backed Hosni Mubarak dictatorship was, might open the Rafah Crossing, Gaza's sole access to the outside that is not subject to direct Israeli control. There has been a slight opening, but not much.

The journalist Laila el-Haddad writes that the reopening under Morsi "is simply a return to status quo of years past: Only Palestinians carrying an Israeli-approved Gaza ID card can use Rafah Crossing." This excludes a great many Palestinians, including el-Haddad's own family, where only one spouse has a card.

Furthermore, she continues, "the crossing does not lead to the West Bank, nor does it allow for the passage of goods, which are restricted to the Israeli-controlled crossings and subject to prohibitions on construction materials and export."

The restricted Rafah Crossing doesn't change the fact that "Gaza remains under tight maritime and aerial siege, and continues to be closed off to the Palestinians' cultural, economic and academic capitals in the rest of the (Israeli-occupied territories), in violation of U.S.-Israeli obligations under the Oslo Accords."

The effects are painfully evident. The director of the Khan Yunis hospital, who is also chief of surgery, describes with anger and passion how even medicines are lacking, which leaves doctors helpless and patients in agony.

One young woman reports on her late father's illness. Though he would have been proud that she was the first woman in the refugee camp to gain an advanced degree, she says, he "passed away after six months of fighting cancer, aged 60 years.

"Israeli occupation denied him a permit to go to Israeli hospitals for treatment. I had to suspend my study, work and life and go to sit next to his bed. We all sat, including my brother the physician and my sister the pharmacist, all powerless and hopeless, watching his suffering. He died during the inhumane blockade of Gaza in summer 2006 with very little access to health service.

"I think feeling powerless and hopeless is the most killing feeling that a human can ever have. It kills the spirit and breaks the heart. You can fight occupation but you cannot fight your feeling of being powerless. You can't even ever dissolve that feeling."

A visitor to Gaza can't help feeling disgust at the obscenity of the occupation, compounded with guilt, because it is within our power to bring the suffering to an end and allow the Samidin to enjoy the lives of peace and dignity that they deserve.

GAZA UNDER ASSAULT

December 1, 2012

An old man in Gaza held a placard that read: "You take my water, burn my olive trees, destroy my house, take my job, steal my land, imprison my father, kill my mother, bombard my country, starve us all, humiliate us all, but I am to blame: I shot a rocket back."

The old man's message provides the proper context for the latest episode in the savage punishment of Gaza. The crimes trace back to 1948, when hundreds of thousands of Palestinians fled from their homes in terror or were expelled to Gaza by conquering Israeli forces, who continued to truck Palestinians over the border for years after the official cease-fire.

The punishment took new forms when Israel conquered Gaza in 1967. From recent Israeli scholarship (primarily Avi Raz's THE BRIDE AND THE DOWRY: ISRAEL, JORDAN, AND THE PALESTINIANS IN THE AFTERMATH OF THE JUNE 1967 WAR), we learn that the government's goal was to drive the refugees into the Sinai Peninsula—and, if feasible, the rest of the population too.

Expulsions from Gaza were carried out under the direct orders of General Yeshayahu Gavish, commander of the Israel Defense Forces Southern Command. Expulsions from the West Bank were far more extreme, and Israel resorted to devious means to prevent the return of those expelled, in direct violation of U.N. Security Council orders.

The reasons were made clear in internal discussions immediately after the war. Golda Meir, later prime minister, informed her Labor Party colleagues that Israel should keep the Gaza Strip while "getting rid of its Arabs." Defense Minister Moshe Dayan and others agreed.

Prime Minister Levi Eshkol explained that those expelled could not be allowed to return because "we cannot increase the Arab population in Israel"—referring to the newly occupied territories, already considered part of Israel.

In accord with this conception, all of Israel's maps were changed, expunging the Green Line (the internationally recognized borders)—though publication of the maps was delayed to permit Abba Eban, an Israeli ambassador to the U.N., to attain what he called a "favorable impasse" at the General Assembly by concealing Israel's intentions.

The goals of expulsion may remain alive today, and might be a factor in contributing to Egypt's reluctance to open the border to free passage of people and goods barred by the U.S.-backed Israeli siege.

The current upsurge of U.S.-Israeli violence dates to January 2006, when Palestinians voted "the wrong way" in the first free election in the Arab world.

Israel and the U.S. reacted at once with harsh punishment of the miscreants, and preparation of a military coup to overthrow the elected government—the routine procedure. The punishment was radically intensified in 2007, when the coup attempt was beaten back and the elected Hamas government established full control over Gaza.

Ignoring immediate offers from Hamas for a truce after the 2006 election, Israel launched attacks that killed 660 Palestinians in 2006, most of whom were civilians (a third were minors). According to U.N. reports, 2,879 Palestinians were killed by Israeli fire from April 2006 through July 2012, along with several dozen Israelis killed by fire from Gaza.

A short-lived truce in 2008 was honored by Hamas until Israel broke it in November. Ignoring further truce offers, Israel launched the murderous Cast Lead operation in December.

So matters have continued, while the U.S. and Israel also continue to reject Hamas calls for a long-term truce and a political settlement for a two-state solution in accord with the international consensus that the U.S. has blocked since 1976 when the U.S. vetoed a U.N. Security Council resolution to this effect, brought by the major Arab states.

This week, Washington devoted every effort to blocking a Palestinian initiative to upgrade its status at the U.N. but failed, in virtual international isolation as usual. The reasons were revealing: Palestine might approach the International Criminal Court about Israel's U.S.-backed crimes.

One element of the unremitting torture of Gaza is Israel's "buffer zone" within Gaza, from which Palestinians are barred entry to almost half of Gaza's limited arable land.

From January 2012 to the launching of Israel's latest killing spree on November 14, Operation Pillar of Defense, one Israeli was killed by fire from Gaza while 78 Palestinians were killed by Israeli fire.

The full story is naturally more complex, and uglier.

The first act of Operation Pillar of Defense was to murder Ahmed Jabari. Aluf Benn, editor of the newspaper *HAARETZ*, describes him as Israel's "subcontractor" and "border guard" in Gaza, who enforced relative quiet there for more than five years.

The pretext for the assassination was that during these five years Jabari had been creating a Hamas military force, with missiles from Iran. A more credible reason was provided by Israeli peace activist Gershon Baskin, who had been involved in direct negotiations with Jabari for years, including plans for the eventual release of the captured Israeli soldier Gilad Shalit.

Baskin reports that hours before he was assassinated, Jabari "received the draft of a permanent truce agreement with Israel, which included mechanisms for maintaining the cease-fire in the case of a flare-up between Israel and the factions in the Gaza Strip."

A truce was then in place, called by Hamas on November 12. Israel apparently exploited the truce, Reuters reports, directing attention to the Syrian border in the hope that Hamas leaders would relax their guard and be easier to assassinate.

Throughout these years, Gaza has been kept on a level of bare survival, imprisoned by land, sea and air. On the eve of the latest attack, the U.N. reported that 40 percent of essential drugs and more than half of essential medical items were out of stock.

In November one of the first in a series of hideous photos sent from Gaza showed a doctor holding the charred corpse of a murdered child. That one had a personal resonance. The doctor is the director and head of surgery at Khan Yunis hospital, which I had visited a few weeks earlier.

In writing about the trip I reported his passionate appeal for desperately needed medicine and surgical equipment. These are among the crimes of the U.S.-Israeli siege, and of Egyptian complicity.

The casualty rates from the November episode were about average: more than 160 Palestinian dead, including many children, and six Israelis.

Among the dead were three journalists. The official Israeli justification was that "the targets are people who have relevance to terror activity." Reporting the "execution" in the *NEW YORK TIMES*, the reporter David Carr observed that "it has come to this: Killing members of the news media can be justified by a phrase as amorphous as 'relevance to terror activity.'"

The massive destruction was all in Gaza. Israel used advanced U.S. military equipment and relied on U.S. diplomatic support, including the usual U.S. intervention efforts to block a Security Council call for a cease-fire.

With each such exploit, Israel's global image erodes. The photos and videos of terror and devastation, and the character of the conflict, leave few remaining shreds of credibility to the self-declared "most moral army in the world," at least among people whose eyes are open.

The pretexts for the assault were also the usual ones. We can put aside the predictable declarations of the perpetrators in Israel and Washington. But even decent people ask what Israel should do when attacked by a barrage of missiles. It's a fair question, and there are straightforward answers.

One response would be to observe international law, which allows the use of force without Security Council authorization in exactly one case: in self-defense after informing the Security Council of an armed attack, until the Council acts, in accord with the U.N. Charter, Article 51.

Israel is well familiar with that Charter provision, which it invoked at the outbreak of the June 1967 war. But, of course, Israel's appeal went nowhere when it was quickly ascertained that Israel had launched the attack. Israel did not follow this course in November, knowing what would be revealed in a Security Council debate.

Another narrow response would be to agree to a truce, as appeared quite possible before the operation was launched on November 14.

There are more far-reaching responses. By coincidence, one is discussed in the current issue of the journal *NATIONAL INTEREST*. Asia scholars Raffaello Pantucci and Alexandros Petersen describe China's reaction after rioting in western Xinjiang province, "in which mobs of Uighurs marched around the city beating hapless Han (Chinese) to death."

Chinese president Hu Jintao quickly flew to the province

to take charge; senior leaders in the security establishment were fired; and a wide range of development projects were undertaken to address underlying causes of the unrest.

In Gaza, too, a civilized reaction is possible. The U.S. and Israel could end the merciless, unremitting assault, open the borders and provide for reconstruction—and if it were imaginable, reparations for decades of violence and repression.

The cease-fire agreement stated that the measures to implement the end of the siege and the targeting of residents in border areas "shall be dealt with after 24 hours from the start of the cease-fire."

There is no sign of steps in this direction. Nor is there any indication of a U.S.-Israeli willingness to rescind their separation of Gaza from the West Bank in violation of the Oslo Accords, to end the illegal settlement and development programs in the West Bank that are designed to undermine a political settlement, or in any other way to abandon the rejectionism of the past decades.

Someday, and it must be soon, the world will respond to the plea issued by the distinguished Gazan human-rights lawyer Raji Sourani while the bombs were once again raining down on defenseless civilians in Gaza: "We demand justice and accountability. We dream of a normal life, in freedom and dignity."

THE GRAVEST THREAT TO WORLD PEACE

January 3, 2013

Reporting on the final U.S. presidential campaign debate, the *WALL STREET JOURNAL* observed that on foreign policy "the only country mentioned more (than Israel) was Iran, which is seen by most nations in the Middle East as the gravest security threat to the region."

The two candidates agreed that a nuclear Iran is the gravest threat to the region, if not the world, as Mitt Romney explicitly maintained, reiterating a conventional view.

On Israel, the candidates vied in declaring their devotion to it, but Israeli officials were nevertheless unsatisfied. They had "hoped for more 'aggressive' language from Mr. Romney," according to the reporters. It was not enough that Romney demanded that Iran not be permitted to "reach a point of nuclear capability."

Arabs were dissatisfied too, because Arab fears about Iran were "debated through the lens of Israeli security instead of the region's," while Arab concerns were largely ignored—again the conventional treatment.

The *WALL STREET JOURNAL* article, like countless others on Iran, leaves critical questions unanswered, among them: Who exactly sees Iran as the gravest security threat? And what do Arabs (and most of the world) think can be done about the threat, whatever they take it to be?

The first question is easily answered. The "Iranian threat" is overwhelmingly a Western obsession, shared by Arab dictators, though not Arab populations.

As numerous polls have shown, although citizens of Arab countries generally dislike Iran, they do not regard it as a very serious threat. Rather, they perceive the threat to be Israel and the United States; and many, sometimes considerable majorities, regard Iranian nuclear weapons as a counter to these threats.

In high places in the United States, some concur with the Arab populations' perception, among them General Lee Butler, former head of the Strategic Command. In 1998 he said, "It is dangerous in the extreme that in the cauldron of animosities that we call the Middle East," one nation, Israel, should have a powerful nuclear weapons arsenal, which "inspires other nations to do so."

Still more dangerous is the nuclear-deterrent strategy of which Butler was a leading designer for many years. Such a strategy, he wrote in 2002, is "a formula for unmitigated catastrophe," and he called on the United States and other nuclear powers to accept their commitment under the Nuclear Non-Proliferation Treaty (NPT) to make "good faith" efforts to eliminate the plague of nuclear weapons.

Nations have a legal obligation to pursue such efforts seriously, the World Court ruled in 1996: "There exists an obligation to pursue in good faith and bring to a conclusion negotiations leading to nuclear disarmament in all its aspects under strict and effective international control." In 2002, George W. Bush's administration declared that the United States is not bound by the obligation.

A large majority of the world appears to share Arab views on the Iranian threat. The Non-Aligned Movement (NAM) has vigorously supported Iran's right to enrich uranium, most recently at its summit meeting in Tehran last August.

India, the most populous member of the Non-Aligned Movement, has found ways to evade the onerous U.S. financial sanctions on Iran. Plans are proceeding to link Iran's Chabahar port, refurbished with Indian assistance, to Central Asia through Afghanistan. Trade relations are also reported to be increasing. Were it not for strong U.S.

pressures, these natural relations would probably improve substantially.

China, which has observer status at the Non-Aligned Movement, is doing much the same. China is expanding development projects westward, including initiatives to reconstitute the old Silk Road from China to Europe. A high-speed rail line connects China to Kazakhstan and beyond. The line will presumably reach Turkmenistan, with its rich energy resources, and will probably link with Iran and extend to Turkey and Europe.

China has also taken over the major Gwadar port in Pakistan, enabling it to obtain oil from the Middle East while avoiding the Hormuz and Malacca straits, which are clogged with traffic and U.S.-controlled. The Pakistani press reports that "crude oil imports from Iran, the Arab Gulf states and Africa could be transported overland to northwest China through the port."

At its Tehran summit in August, the Non-Aligned Movement reiterated the long-standing proposal to mitigate or end the threat of nuclear weapons in the Middle East by establishing a zone free of weapons of mass destruction. Moves in that direction are clearly the most straightforward and least onerous way to overcome the threats. They are supported by almost the entire world.

A fine opportunity to carry such measures forward arose last month, when an international conference was planned on the matter in Helsinki.

A conference did take place, but not the one that was planned. Only nongovernmental organizations participated in the alternate conference, hosted by the Peace Union of Finland. The planned international conference was canceled by Washington in November, shortly after Iran agreed to attend.

The Obama administration's official reason was "political turmoil in the region and Iran's defiant stance on nonpro-liferation," the Associated Press reported, along with lack of consensus "on how to approach the conference." That reason is the approved reference to the fact that the region's only nuclear power, Israel, refused to attend, calling the request to do so "coercion."

Apparently, the Obama administration is keeping to its earlier position that "conditions are not right unless all members of the region participate." The United States will not allow measures to place Israel's nuclear facilities under international inspection. Nor will the U.S. release informa-tion on "the nature and scope of Israeli nuclear facilities and activities."

The Kuwait news agency immediately reported that "the Arab group of states and the Non-Aligned Movement mem-ber states agreed to continue lobbying for a conference on establishing a Middle East zone free of nuclear weapons and all other weapons of mass destruction."

Last month, the U.N. General Assembly passed a resolu-tion calling on Israel to join the NPT, 174–6. Voting no was the usual contingent: Israel, the United States, Canada, Mar-shall Islands, Micronesia and Palau.

A few days later, the United States carried out a nuclear weapons test, again banning international inspectors from the test site in Nevada. Iran protested, as did the mayor of Hiro-shima and some Japanese peace groups.

Establishment of a nuclear weapons–free zone of course requires the cooperation of the nuclear powers: in the Middle East, that would include the United States and Israel, which refuse. The same is true elsewhere. Such zones in Africa and the Pacific await implementation because the U.S. insists on maintaining and upgrading nuclear weapons bases on islands it controls.

As the NGO meeting convened in Helsinki, a dinner took place in New York under the auspices of the Washington Institute for Near East Policy, an offshoot of the Israeli lobby.

According to an enthusiastic report on the "gala" in the Israeli press, Dennis Ross, Elliott Abrams and other "former top advisers to Obama and Bush" assured the audience that "the president will strike (Iran) next year if diplomacy doesn't succeed"—a most attractive holiday gift.

Americans can hardly be aware of how diplomacy has once again failed, for a simple reason: Virtually nothing is reported in the United States about the fate of the most obvious way to address "the gravest threat": establish a nuclear weapons–free zone in the Middle East.

WHO OWNS THE WORLD?

February 5, 2013

EXCERPTED FROM *POWER SYSTEMS: CONVERSATIONS ON GLOBAL DEMOCRATIC UPRISINGS AND THE NEW CHALLENGES TO U.S. EMPIRE. INTERVIEWS WITH DAVID BARSAMIAN BY NOAM CHOMSKY.*

DAVID BARSAMIAN: The new American imperialism seems to be substantially different from the older variety in that the United States is a declining economic power and is therefore seeing its political power and influence wane.

NOAM CHOMSKY: I think talk about American decline should be taken with a grain of salt.

World War II is when the United States really became a global power. It had been the biggest economy in the world by far for long before the war, but it was a regional power in a way. It controlled the Western Hemisphere and had made some forays into the Pacific. But the British were the world power.

World War II changed that. The United States became the dominant world power. The U.S. had half the world's wealth. The other industrial societies were weakened or destroyed. The U.S. was in an incredible position of security. It controlled the hemisphere, and both the Atlantic and the Pacific, with a huge military force.

Of course, that declined. Europe and Japan recovered, and decolonization took place. By 1970, the U.S. was down, if you want to call it that, to about 25 percent of the world's wealth—roughly what it had been, say, in the 1920s. It remained the overwhelming global power, but not like it had been in 1950. Since 1970, it's been pretty stable, though of course there were changes.

Within the last decade, for the first time in 500 years, since the Spanish and Portuguese conquest, Latin America has begun to deal with some of its problems. It's begun to integrate. The countries were very separated from one another. Each one was oriented separately toward the West, first Europe and then the United States.

That integration is important. It means that it's not so easy to pick off the countries one by one. Latin American nations can unify in defense against an outside force.

The other development, which is more significant and much more difficult, is that the countries of Latin America are individually beginning to face their massive internal problems. With its resources, Latin America ought to be a rich continent, South America particularly.

Latin America has a huge amount of wealth, but it is very highly concentrated in a small, usually Europeanized, often white elite, and exists alongside massive poverty and misery. There are some attempts to begin to deal with that, which is important—another form of integration—and Latin America is somewhat separating itself from U.S. control.

There's a lot of talk about a global shift of power: India and China are going to become the new great powers, the wealthiest powers. Again, one should be pretty reserved about that.

For example, many observers comment about U.S. debt and the fact that China holds so much of it. A few years ago, actually, Japan held most of the U.S. debt, now surpassed by China.

Furthermore, the whole framework for the discussion of U.S. decline is misleading. We're taught to talk about a world of states conceived as unified, coherent entities.

If you study international relations theory, there's what's called the "realist" school, which says there is an anarchic world of states, and those states pursue their "national interest." It's in large part mythology. There are a few common interests, like survival. But, for the most part, people within a nation have very different interests. The interests of the CEO of General Electric and the janitor who cleans his floor are not the same.

Part of the doctrinal system in the United States is the pretense that we're all a happy family, there are no class divisions, and everybody is working together in harmony. But that's radically false.

In the 18th century, Adam Smith said that the people who own the society make policy: the "merchants and manufacturers." Today power is in the hands of financial institutions and multinationals.

These institutions have an interest in Chinese development. So if you're, say, the CEO of Walmart or Dell or Hewlett-Packard, you're perfectly happy to have very cheap labor in China working under hideous conditions and with few environmental constraints. As long as China has what's called economic growth, that's fine.

Actually, China's economic growth is a bit of a myth. China is largely an assembly plant. China is a major exporter, but while the U.S. trade deficit with China has gone up, the trade deficit with Japan, Taiwan and Korea has gone down. The reason is that a regional production system is developing.

The more advanced countries of the region—Japan, Singapore, South Korea and Taiwan—send advanced technology, parts and components to China, which uses its cheap labor force to assemble goods and send them out of the country.

And U.S. corporations do the same thing: They send parts and components to China, where people assemble and export the final products. These are called Chinese exports, but they're regional exports in many instances, and in other instances it's actually a case of the United States exporting to itself.

Once we break out of the framework of national states as unified entities with no internal divisions within them, we can see that there is a global shift of power, but it's from the global workforce to the owners of the world: transnational capital, global financial institutions.

CAN CIVILIZATION SURVIVE CAPITALISM?

March 4, 2013

There is "capitalism" and then there is "really existing capitalism."

The term "capitalism" is commonly used to refer to the U.S. economic system, with substantial state intervention ranging from subsidies for creative innovation to the "too-big-to-fail" government insurance policy for banks.

The system is highly monopolized, further limiting reliance on the market, and increasingly so: In the past 20 years the share of profits of the 200 largest enterprises has risen sharply, reports scholar Robert W. McChesney in his new book, DIGITAL DISCONNECT.

"Capitalism" is a term now commonly used to describe systems in which there are no capitalists: for example, the worker-owned Mondragon conglomerate in the Basque region of Spain, or the worker-owned enterprises expanding in northern Ohio, often with conservative support—both are discussed in important work by the scholar Gar Alperovitz.

Some might even use the term "capitalism" to refer to the industrial democracy advocated by John Dewey, America's leading social philosopher, in the late 19th century and early 20th century.

Dewey called for workers to be "masters of their own industrial fate" and for all institutions to be brought under public control, including the means of production, exchange, publicity, transportation and communication. Short of this, Dewey argued, politics will remain "the shadow cast on society by big business."

The truncated democracy that Dewey condemned has been left in tatters in recent years. Now control of government is narrowly concentrated at the peak of the income

scale, while the large majority "down below" has been virtually disenfranchised. The current political-economic system
is a form of plutocracy, diverging sharply from democracy,
if by that concept we mean political arrangements in which
policy is significantly influenced by the public will.

There have been serious debates over the years about
whether capitalism is compatible with democracy. If we keep
to really existing capitalist democracy the question is effectively answered: They are radically incompatible.

It seems to me unlikely that civilization can survive really
existing capitalism and the sharply attenuated democracy that
goes along with it. But could functioning democracy make a
difference?

Let's keep to the most critical immediate problem that
civilization faces: environmental catastrophe. Policies and
public attitudes diverge sharply, as is often the case under
really existing capitalist democracy. The nature of the gap is
examined in several articles in the current issue of *DAEDALUS*,
the journal of the American Academy of Arts and Sciences.

Researcher Kelly Sims Gallagher finds that "one hundred and nine countries have enacted some form of policy
regarding renewable power, and 118 countries have set targets for renewable energy. In contrast, the United States has
not adopted any consistent and stable set of policies at the
national level to foster the use of renewable energy."

It is not public opinion that drives American policy off
the international spectrum. Quite the opposite. Opinion is
much closer to the global norm than the U.S. government's
policies reflect, and much more supportive of actions needed
to confront the likely environmental disaster predicted by an
overwhelming scientific consensus—and one that's not too far
off, affecting the lives of our grandchildren, very likely.

As Jon A. Krosnick and Bo MacInnis report in *DAEDALUS*:

"Huge majorities have favored steps by the federal government to reduce the amount of greenhouse gas emissions generated when utilities produce electricity. In 2006, 86 percent of respondents favored requiring utilities, or encouraging them with tax breaks, to reduce the amount of greenhouse gases they emit. . . . Also in that year, 87 percent favored tax breaks for utilities that produce more electricity from water, wind or sunlight. . . . These majorities were maintained between 2006 and 2010 and shrank somewhat after that. . . ."

The fact that the public is influenced by science is deeply troubling to those who dominate the economy and state policy.

One current illustration of their concern is the "Environmental Literacy Improvement Act" proposed to state legislatures by ALEC, the American Legislative Exchange Council, a corporate-funded lobby that designs legislation to serve the needs of the corporate sector and extreme wealth.

The ALEC Act mandates "balanced teaching" of climate science in K–12 classrooms. "Balanced teaching" is a code phrase that refers to teaching climate-change denial, to "balance" mainstream climate science. It is analogous to the "balanced teaching" advocated by creationists to enable the teaching of "creation science" in public schools. Legislation based on ALEC models has already been introduced in several states.

Of course, all of this is dressed up in rhetoric about teaching critical thinking—a fine idea, no doubt, but it's easy to think up far better examples than an issue that threatens our survival and has been selected because of its importance in terms of corporate profits.

Media reports commonly present a controversy between two sides on climate change.

One side consists of the overwhelming majority of scientists, the world's major national academies of science, the professional science journals and the Intergovernmental Panel on Climate Change (IPCC).

They agree that global warming is taking place, that there is a substantial human component, that the situation is serious and perhaps dire, and that very soon, maybe within decades, the world might reach a tipping point where the process will escalate sharply and will be irreversible, with severe social and economic effects. It is rare to find such consensus on complex scientific issues.

The other side consists of skeptics, including a few respected scientists who caution that much is unknown—which means that things might not be as bad as thought, or they might be worse.

Omitted from the contrived debate is a much larger group of skeptics: highly regarded climate scientists who see the IPCC's regular reports as much too conservative. And these scientists have repeatedly been proven correct, unfortunately.

The propaganda campaign has apparently had some effect on U.S. public opinion, which is more skeptical than the global norm. But the effect is not significant enough to satisfy the masters. That is presumably why sectors of the corporate world are launching their attack on the educational system, in an effort to counter the public's dangerous tendency to pay attention to the conclusions of scientific research.

At the Republican National Committee's Winter Meeting a few weeks ago, Louisiana Governor Bobby Jindal warned the leadership that "we must stop being the stupid party. . . . We must stop insulting the intelligence of voters."

Within the system of really existing capitalist democracy it is of extreme importance that we become the stupid nation, not misled by science and rationality, in the interests of the short-term gains of the masters of the economy and political system, and damn the consequences.

These commitments are deeply rooted in the fundamentalist market doctrines that are preached within really existing capitalist democracy, though observed in a highly selective manner, so as to sustain a powerful state that serves wealth and power.

The official doctrines suffer from a number of familiar "market inefficiencies," among them the failure to take into account the effects on others in market transactions. The consequences of these "externalities" can be substantial. The current financial crisis is an illustration. It is partly traceable to the major banks and investment firms' ignoring "systemic risk"—the possibility that the whole system would collapse—when they undertook risky transactions.

Environmental catastrophe is far more serious: The externality that is being ignored is the fate of the species. And there is nowhere to run, cap in hand, for a bailout.

In the future, historians (if there are any) will look back on this curious spectacle taking shape in the early 21st century. For the first time in human history, humans are facing the significant prospect of severe calamity as a result of their actions—actions that are battering our prospects of decent survival.

Those historians will observe that the richest and most powerful country in history, which enjoys incomparable advantages, is leading the effort to intensify the likely disaster. Leading the effort to preserve conditions in which our immediate descendants might have a decent life are the so-called "primitive" societies: First Nations, tribal, indigenous, aboriginal.

The countries with large and influential indigenous populations are well in the lead in seeking to preserve the planet. The countries that have driven indigenous populations to extinction or extreme marginalization are racing toward destruction.

Thus Ecuador, with its large indigenous population, is seeking aid from the rich countries to allow it to keep its substantial oil reserves underground, where they should be.

Meanwhile the U.S. and Canada are seeking to burn fossil fuels, including the extremely dangerous Canadian tar sands, and to do so as quickly and fully as possible, while they hail the wonders of a century of (largely meaningless) energy independence without a side glance at what the world might look like after this extravagant commitment to self-destruction.

This observation generalizes: Throughout the world, indigenous societies are struggling to protect what they sometimes call "the rights of nature," while the civilized and sophisticated scoff at this silliness.

This is all exactly the opposite of what rationality would predict—unless it is the skewed form of reason that passes through the filter of really existing capitalist democracy.

IN PALESTINE, DIGNITY AND VIOLENCE
April 1, 2013

THIS ARTICLE IS ADAPTED FROM THE EDWARD W. SAID LECTURE GIVEN BY NOAM CHOMSKY IN LONDON ON MARCH 18, 2013.

The Swedish novelist Henning Mankell tells of an experience in Mozambique during the civil war horrors there 25 years ago, when he saw a young man walking toward him in ragged clothes.

"I noticed something that I will never forget for as long as I live," Mankell says. "I looked at his feet. He had no shoes. Instead he had painted shoes on his feet. He had used the colors in the ground and in the roots to replace his shoes. He had come up with a way to keep his dignity."

Such scenes will evoke poignant memories among those who have witnessed cruelty and degradation, which are everywhere. One striking case, though only one of a great many, is Gaza, which I was able to visit for the first time last October.

There violence is met by the steady resistance of the Samidin—those who endure, to borrow Raja Shehadeh's evocative term in *THE THIRD WAY*, his memoir on Palestinians under occupation, published 30 years ago.

Greeting me on my return home were the reports of the Israeli assault on Gaza in November, supported by the United States and tolerated politely by Europe as usual.

Israel isn't Gaza's only adversary. Gaza's southern border remains largely under the control of Egypt's dreaded secret police, the Mukhabarat, which credible reports link closely to the CIA and the Israeli Mossad.

Just last month a young Gaza journalist sent me an article describing the Egyptian government's latest assault on the people of Gaza.

A network of tunnels into Egypt is a lifeline for Gazans imprisoned under harsh siege and constant attack. Now the Egyptian government has devised a new way to block the tunnels: flooding them with sewage.

Meanwhile the Israeli human rights group B'Tselem reports on a new device that the Israeli army is using to counter the weekly nonviolent protests against Israel's illegal Separation Wall—in reality an Annexation Wall.

The Samidin have been ingenious in coping with tear gas so the army has escalated, spraying protesters and homes with jets of a liquid as noxious as raw sewage.

These attacks provide more evidence that great minds think alike, combining criminal repression with humiliation.

The tragedy of Gaza traces back to 1948, when hundreds of thousands of Palestinians fled in terror or were forcibly expelled to Gaza by conquering Israeli forces.

Prime Minister David Ben-Gurion held that "the Arabs of the Land of Israel have only one function left to them—to run away."

It is noteworthy that today the strongest support for Israel in the international arena comes from the United States, Canada and Australia, the so-called Anglosphere—settler-colonial societies based on extermination or expulsion of indigenous populations in favor of a higher race, and where such behavior is considered natural and praiseworthy.

For decades Gaza has been a showcase for violence of every kind. The record includes such carefully planned atrocities as Operation Cast Lead in 2008–2009—"infanticide," as it was called by Norwegian physicians Mads Gilbert and Erik Fosse, who worked at Gaza's al-Shifa Hospital with their Palestinian and Norwegian colleagues through the criminal assault. The word is apt, considering the hundreds of children massacred.

Violence ranges through just about every kind of cruelty that humans have used their higher mental faculties to devise, up to the pain of exile.

The pain is particularly stark in Gaza, where older people can still look across the border toward the homes from which they were driven—or could if they were able to approach the border without being killed.

One form of punishment has been to close off more of the Gazan side of the border, turning it into a buffer zone, including half of Gaza's arable land, according to Harvard's Sara Roy, a leading scholar on Gaza.

While a showcase for the human capacity for violence, Gaza is also an inspiring exemplar of the demand for dignity.

Ghada Ageel, a young woman who escaped from Gaza to Canada, writes about her 87-year-old refugee grandmother, still trapped in the Gaza prison. Before her grandmother's expulsion from a now-destroyed village, "she owned a house, farms and land and she enjoyed honor, dignity and hope."

Amazingly, like Palestinians generally, the elderly woman hasn't given up hope.

"When I saw my grandmother in November 2012 she was unusually happy," Ageel writes. "Surprised by her high spirits, I asked for an explanation. She looked me in the eye and, to my surprise, said that she was no longer worried about" her native village and the life of dignity that she has lost, for her irrevocably.

The village, her grandmother told Ageel, "is in your heart, and I also know that you are not alone in your journey. Don't be discouraged. We are getting there."

The search for dignity is understood instinctively by those who hold the clubs, and who recognize that apart from violence, the best way to undermine dignity is by humiliation. That is second nature in prisons.

The normal practice in Israeli prisons is once again under scrutiny. In February, Arafat Jaradat, a 30-year-old gas-station attendant, died in Israeli custody. The circumstances might yet spark another uprising.

Jaradat was arrested in his home at midnight (an appropriate hour to intimidate his family) and charged with having thrown stones and a Molotov cocktail a few months earlier, during Israel's November attack on Gaza.

Jaradat, healthy when arrested, was last seen alive in court by his lawyer, who describes him as "doubled over, scared, confused and shrunken."

The court remanded him to another 12 days of detention. Jaradat was found dead in his cell.

Journalist Amira Hass writes that "the Palestinians do not need an Israeli investigation. For them, Jaradat's death is much bigger than the tragedy he and his family have suffered. From their experience, Jaradat's death is . . . proof that the Israeli system routinely uses torture. From their experience, the goal of torture is not only to convict someone, but mainly to deter and subjugate an entire people."

The means are humiliation, degradation and terror—familiar features of repression at home and abroad.

The need to humiliate those who raise their heads is an ineradicable element of the imperial mentality.

In the case of Israel-Palestine, there has long been a near-unanimous international consensus on a diplomatic settlement, blocked by the United States for 35 years, with tacit European acceptance.

Contempt for the worthless victims is no small part of the barrier to achieving a settlement with at least a modicum of justice and respect for human dignity and rights. It's not beyond imagination that the barrier can be overcome by dedicated work, as has been done elsewhere.

Unless the powerful are capable of learning to respect the dignity of the victims, impassable barriers will remain, and the world will be doomed to violence, cruelty and bitter suffering.

BOSTON AND BEYOND
May 1, 2013

April is usually a cheerful month in New England, with the first signs of spring, and the harsh winter at last receding. Not this year.

There are few in Boston who were not touched in some way by the marathon bombings on April 15 and the tense week that followed. Several friends of mine were at the finish line when the bombs went off. Others live close to where Dzhokhar Tsarnaev, the second suspect, was captured. The young police officer Sean Collier was murdered right outside my office building.

It's rare for privileged Westerners to see, graphically, what many others experience daily—for example, in a remote village in Yemen, the same week as the marathon bombings.

On April 23, Yemeni activist and journalist Farea Al-Muslimi, who had studied at an American high school, testified before a U.S. Senate committee that right after the marathon bombings, a drone strike in his home village in Yemen killed its target.

The strike terrorized the villagers, turning them into enemies of the United States—something that years of jihadi propaganda had failed to accomplish.

His neighbors had admired the United States, Al-Muslimi told the committee, but "now, however, when they think of America, they think of the fear they feel at the drones over their heads. What radicals had previously failed to achieve in my village, one drone strike accomplished in an instant."

Rack up another triumph for President Obama's global assassination program, which creates hatred of the United States and threats to its citizens more rapidly than it kills people who are suspected of posing a possible danger to us someday.

The target of the Yemeni village assassination—which was carried out to induce maximum terror in the population—was well-known and could easily have been apprehended, Al-Muslimi said. This is another familiar feature of the global terror operations.

There was no direct way to prevent the Boston murders. There are some easy ways to prevent likely future ones: by not inciting them. That's also true of another case of a suspect murdered, his body disposed of without autopsy, when he could easily have been apprehended and brought to trial: Osama bin Laden.

This murder too had consequences. To locate bin Laden, the CIA launched a fraudulent vaccination campaign in a poor neighborhood, then switched it, uncompleted, to a richer area where the suspect was thought to be.

The CIA operation violated fundamental principles as old as the Hippocratic oath. It also endangered health workers associated with a polio vaccination program in Pakistan, several of whom were abducted and killed, prompting the U.N. to withdraw its anti-polio team.

The CIA ruse also will lead to the deaths of unknown numbers of Pakistanis who have been deprived of protection from polio because they fear that foreign killers may still be exploiting vaccination programs.

Columbia University health scientist Leslie Roberts estimated that 100,000 cases of polio may follow this incident; he told SCIENTIFIC AMERICAN that "people would say this disease, this crippled child is because the U.S. was so crazy to get Osama bin Laden."

And they may choose to react, as aggrieved people sometimes do, in ways that will cause their tormentors consternation and outrage.

Even more severe consequences were narrowly averted.

The U.S. Navy SEALs were under orders to fight their way out if necessary. Pakistan has a well-trained army, committed to defending the state. Had the invaders been confronted, Washington would not have left them to their fate. Rather, the full force of the U.S. killing machine might have been used to extricate them, quite possibly leading to nuclear war.

There is a long and highly instructive history showing the willingness of state authorities to risk the fate of their populations, sometimes severely, for the sake of their policy objectives, not least the most powerful state in the world. We ignore it at our peril.

There is no need to ignore it right now. A remedy is investigative reporter Jeremy Scahill's just-published *DIRTY WARS: THE WORLD IS A BATTLEFIELD*.

In chilling detail, Scahill describes the effects on the ground of U.S. military operations, terror strikes from the air (drones), and the exploits of the secret army of the executive branch, the Joint Special Operations Command, which rapidly expanded under President George W. Bush, then became a weapon of choice for President Obama.

We should bear in mind an astute observation by the author and activist Fred Branfman, who almost single-handedly exposed the true horrors of the U.S. "secret wars" in Laos in the 1960s, and their extensions beyond.

Considering today's JSOC-CIA-drones/killing machines, Branfman reminds us about the Senate testimony in 1969 of Monteagle Stearns, U.S. deputy chief of mission in Laos from 1969 to 1972.

Asked why the U.S. rapidly escalated its bombing after President Johnson had ordered a halt over North Vietnam in November 1968, Stearns said, "Well, we had all those planes sitting around and couldn't just let them stay there with nothing to do"—so we can use them to drive poor peasants in remote villages of northern Laos into caves to survive, even penetrating within the caves with our advanced technology.

JSOC and the drones are a self-generating terror machine that will grow and expand, meanwhile creating new potential targets as they sweep much of the world. And the executive won't want them just "sitting around."

It wouldn't hurt to contemplate another slice of history, at the dawn of the 20th century.

In his book POLICING AMERICA'S EMPIRE: THE UNITED STATES, THE PHILIPPINES AND THE RISE OF THE SURVEILLANCE STATE, the historian Alfred McCoy explores in depth the U.S. pacification of the Philippines after an invasion that killed hundreds of thousands through savagery and torture.

The conquerors established a sophisticated surveillance and control system, using the most advanced technology of the day to ensure obedience, with consequences for the Philippines that reach to the present.

And as McCoy demonstrates, it wasn't long before the successes found their way home, where such methods were employed to control the domestic population—in softer ways to be sure, but not very attractive ones.

We can expect the same. The dangers of unexamined and unregulated monopoly power, particularly in the state executive, are hardly news. The right reaction is not passive acquiescence.

GUILTY IN GUATEMALA
June 3, 2013

On Mother's Day, May 12, the BOSTON GLOBE featured a photo of a young woman with her toddler son sleeping in her arms.

The woman, of Mayan Indian heritage, had crossed the U.S. border seven times while pregnant, only to be caught and shipped back across the border on six of those attempts. She braved many miles, enduring blisteringly hot days and freezing nights, with no water or shelter, amid roaming gunmen. The last time she crossed, seven months pregnant, she was rescued by immigration solidarity activists who helped her to find her way to Boston.

Most of the border crossers are from Central America. Many say they would rather be home, if the possibility of decent survival hadn't been destroyed. Mayans such as this young mother are still fleeing from the wreckage of the genocidal assault on the indigenous population of the Guatemalan highlands 30 years ago.

The main perpetrator, General Efraín Ríos Montt, the former dictator who ruled Guatemala during two of the bloodiest years of the country's decades-long civil war, was convicted in a Guatemalan court of genocide and crimes against humanity, on May 10.

Then, 10 days later, the case was overturned under suspicious circumstances. It is unclear whether the trial will continue.

Ríos Montt's forces killed tens of thousands of Guatemalans, mostly Mayans, in the year 1982 alone.

As that bloody year ended, President Reagan assured the nation that the killer was "a man of great personal integrity and commitment," who was getting a "bum rap" from human-rights organizations and who "wants to improve the quality of life for all Guatemalans and to promote social justice." Therefore, the president continued, "My administration will do all it can to support his progressive efforts."

Ample evidence of Ríos Montt's "progressive efforts" was available to Washington, not only from rights organizations, but also from U.S. intelligence.

But truth was unwelcome. It interfered with the objectives set by Reagan's national security team in 1981. As reported by the journalist Robert Parry, working from a document he discovered in the Reagan Library, the team's goal was to supply military aid to the right-wing regime in Guatemala in order to exterminate not only "Marxist guerrillas" but also their "civilian support mechanisms"—which means, effectively, genocide.

The task was carried out with dedication. Reagan sent "nonlethal" equipment to the killers, including Bell helicopters that were immediately armed and sent on their missions of death and destruction.

But the most effective method was to enlist a network of client states to take over the task, including Taiwan and South Korea, still under U.S.-backed dictatorships, as well as apartheid South Africa and the Argentine and Chilean dictatorships.

At the forefront was Israel, which became the major arms supplier to Guatemala. It provided instructors for the killers and participated in counterinsurgency operations.

The background bears restating. In 1954, a CIA-run military coup ended a 10-year democratic interlude in Guatemala—"the years of spring," as they are known there—and restored a savage elite to power.

In the 1990s, international organizations conducting inquiries into the fighting reported that since 1954 some 200,000 people had been killed in Guatemala, 80 percent of whom were indigenous. The killers were mostly from the Guatemalan security forces and closely linked paramilitaries.

The atrocities were carried out with vigorous U.S. support and participation. Among the standard Cold War pretexts was that Guatemala was a Russian "beachhead" in Latin America.

The real reasons, amply documented, were also standard: concern for the interests of U.S. investors and fear that a democratic experiment empowering the harshly repressed peasant majority "might be a virus" that would "spread contagion," in Henry Kissinger's thoughtful phrase, referring to Salvador Allende's democratic socialist Chile.

Reagan's murderous assault on Central America was not limited to Guatemala, of course. In most of the region the agencies of terror were government security forces that had been armed and trained by Washington.

One country was different: Nicaragua. It had an army to defend its population. Reagan therefore had to organize right-wing guerrilla forces to wage the fight.

In 1986, the World Court, in *Nicaragua v. United States*, condemned the U.S. for "unlawful use of force" in Nicaragua and ordered the payment of reparations. The United States' response to the court's decree was to escalate the proxy war.

The U.S. Southern Command ordered the guerrillas to attack virtually defenseless civilian targets, not to "duke it out" with the Nicaraguan army, according to Southcom's General John Gavin testimony to Congress in 1987.

Rights organizations (the same ones that were giving a bad rap to genocidaire Ríos Montt) had condemned the war in Nicaragua all along but vehemently protested Southcom's "soft-target" tactics.

The American commentator Michael Kinsley reprimanded the rights organizations for departing from good form. He explained that a "sensible policy" must "meet the test of cost-benefit analysis," evaluating "the amount of blood and misery that will be poured in, and the likelihood that democracy will emerge at the other end."

Naturally, we Americans have the right to conduct the analysis—thanks, presumably, to our inherent nobility and stellar record ever since the days when the continent was cleared of the native scourge.

The nature of the "democracy that will emerge" was hardly obscure. It is accurately described by the leading scholar of "democracy promotion," Thomas Carothers, who worked on such projects in the Reagan State Department.

Carothers concludes, regretfully, that U.S. influence was inversely proportional to democratic progress in Latin America, because Washington would only tolerate "limited, top-down forms of democratic change that did not risk upsetting the traditional structures of power with which the United States has long been allied (in) quite undemocratic societies."

There has been no change since.

In 1999, President Clinton apologized for American crimes in Guatemala, but no action was taken.

There are countries that rise to a higher level than idle apology without action. Guatemala, despite its continuing travails, has carried out the unprecedented act of bringing a former head of state to trial for his crimes, something we might remember on the 10th anniversary of the U.S. invasion of Iraq.

Also perhaps unprecedented is an article in the *NEW YORK TIMES* by Elisabeth Malkin, headlined "Trial on Guatemalan Civil War Carnage Leaves Out U.S. Role." Even acknowledgment of one's own crimes is very rare.

Rare to nonexistent are actions that could alleviate some

of the crimes' horrendous consequences—for example, for the United States to pay the reparations to Nicaragua ordered by the World Court. The absence of such actions provides one measure of the chasm that separates us from where a civilized society ought to be.

WHO OWNS THE EARTH?

July 4, 2013

This article is adapted from a commencement speech by Noam Chomsky on June 14, 2013, at the American University of Beirut.

With wrenching tragedies only a few miles away, and still worse catastrophes perhaps not far removed, it may seem wrong, perhaps even cruel, to shift attention to other prospects that, although abstract and uncertain, might offer a path to a better world—and not in the remote future.

I've visited Lebanon several times and witnessed moments of great hope, and of despair, that were tinged with the Lebanese people's remarkable determination to overcome and to move forward.

The first time I visited—if that's the right word—was exactly 60 years ago, almost to the day. My wife and I were hiking in Israel's northern Galilee one evening, when a jeep drove by on a road near us and someone called out that we should turn back: We were in the wrong country. We had inadvertently crossed the border, then unmarked—now, I suppose, bristling with armaments.

A minor event, but it forcefully brought home a lesson: The legitimacy of borders—of states, for that matter—is at best conditional and temporary.

Almost all borders have been imposed and maintained by violence, and are quite arbitrary. The Lebanon-Israel border was established a century ago by the Sykes-Picot Agreement, dividing up the former Ottoman Empire in the interests of British and French imperial power, with no concern for the people who happened to live there, or even for the terrain.

The border makes no sense, which is why it was so easy to cross unwittingly.

Surveying the terrible conflicts in the world, it's clear that almost all are the residue of imperial crimes and the borders that the great powers drew in their own interests.

Pashtuns, for example, have never accepted the legitimacy of the Durand Line, drawn by Britain to separate Pakistan from Afghanistan; nor has any Afghan government ever accepted it. It is in the interests of today's imperial powers that Pashtuns crossing the Durand Line are labeled "terrorists" so that their homes may be subjected to murderous attack by U.S. drones and special operations forces.

Few borders in the world are so heavily guarded by sophisticated technology, and so subject to impassioned rhetoric, as the one that separates Mexico from the United States, two countries with amicable diplomatic relations.

That border was established by U.S. aggression during the 19th century. But it was kept fairly open until 1994, when President Bill Clinton initiated Operation Gatekeeper, militarizing it.

Before then, people had regularly crossed it to see relatives and friends. It's likely that Operation Gatekeeper was motivated by another event that year: the imposition of the North American Free Trade Agreement, which is a misnomer because of the words "free trade."

Doubtless the Clinton administration understood that Mexican farmers, however efficient they might be, couldn't compete with highly subsidized U.S. agribusiness, and that Mexican businesses couldn't compete with U.S. multinationals, which under NAFTA rules must receive special privileges like "national treatment" in Mexico. Such measures would almost inevitably lead to a flood of immigrants across the border.

Some borders are eroding along with the cruel hatreds

and conflicts they symbolize and inspire. The most dramatic case is Europe. For centuries, Europe was the most savage region in the world, torn by hideous and destructive wars. Europe developed the technology and the culture of war that enabled it to conquer the world. After a final burst of indescribable savagery, the mutual destruction ceased at the end of World War II.

Scholars attribute that outcome to the thesis of democratic peace—that one democracy hesitates to war against another. But Europeans may also have understood that they had developed such capacities for destruction that the next time they played their favorite game, it would be the last.

The closer integration that has developed since then is not without serious problems, but it is a vast improvement over what came before.

A similar outcome would hardly be unprecedented for the Middle East, which until recently was essentially borderless. And the borders are eroding, though in awful ways.

Syria's seemingly inexorable plunge to suicide is tearing the country apart. Veteran Middle East correspondent Patrick Cockburn, now working for the *INDEPENDENT*, predicts that the conflagration and its regional impact may lead to the end of the Sykes-Picot regime.

The Syrian civil war has reignited the Sunni-Shiite conflict that was one of the most terrible consequences of the U.S.-U.K. invasion of Iraq 10 years ago.

The Kurdish regions of Iraq and now Syria are moving toward autonomy and linkages. Many analysts now predict that a Kurdish state may be established before a Palestinian state is.

If Palestine ever gains independence in something like the terms of the overwhelming international consensus, its borders with Israel will likely erode through normal commercial and cultural interchange, as has happened in the past during periods of relative calm.

That development could be a step toward closer regional integration, and perhaps the slow disappearance of the artificial border dividing the Galilee between Israel and Lebanon, so that hikers and others could pass freely where my wife and I crossed 60 years ago.

Such a development seems to me to offer the only realistic hope for some resolution of the plight of Palestinian refugees, now only one of the refugee disasters tormenting the region since the invasion of Iraq and Syria's descent into hell.

The blurring of borders and these challenges to the legitimacy of states bring to the fore serious questions about who owns the Earth. Who owns the global atmosphere being polluted by the heat-trapping gases that have just passed an especially perilous threshold, as we learned in May?

Or, to adopt the phrase used by indigenous people throughout much of the world, Who will defend the Earth? Who will uphold the rights of nature? Who will adopt the role of steward of the commons, our collective possession?

That the Earth now desperately needs defense from impending environmental catastrophe is surely obvious to any rational and literate person. The different reactions to the crisis are a most remarkable feature of current history.

At the forefront of the defense of nature are those often called "primitive": members of indigenous and tribal groups, like the First Nations in Canada or the Aborigines in Australia—the remnants of peoples who have survived the imperial onslaught. At the forefront of the assault on nature are those who call themselves the most advanced and civilized: the richest and most powerful nations.

The struggle to defend the commons takes many forms. In microcosm, it is taking place right now in Turkey's Taksim

Square, where brave men and women are protecting one of the last remnants of the commons of Istanbul from the wrecking ball of commercialization and gentrification and autocratic rule that is destroying this ancient treasure.

The defenders of Taksim Square are at the forefront of a worldwide struggle to preserve the global commons from the ravages of that same wrecking ball—a struggle in which we must all take part, with dedication and resolve, if there is to be any hope for decent human survival in a world that has no borders. It is our common possession, to defend or to destroy.

IS EDWARD J. SNOWDEN ABOARD
THIS PLANE?

July 31, 2013

On July 9, the Organization of American States (OAS) held a special session to discuss the shocking behavior of the European states that had refused to allow the government plane carrying Bolivian president Evo Morales to enter their airspace.

Morales was flying home from a Moscow summit on July 3. In an interview there he had said he was open to offering political asylum to Edward J. Snowden, the former U.S. spy-agency contractor wanted by Washington on espionage charges, who was in the Moscow airport.

The OAS expressed its solidarity with Morales, condemned "actions that violate the basic rules and principles of international law such as the inviolability of Heads of State," and "firmly" called on the European governments—France, Italy, Portugal and Spain—to explain their actions and issue apologies.

An emergency meeting of UNASUR—the Union of South American Nations—denounced "the flagrant violation of international treaties" by European powers.

Latin American heads of state weighed in, too. President Dilma Rousseff of Brazil expressed the country's "indignation and condemnation of the situation imposed on President Evo Morales by some European countries" and warned that this "serious lack of respect for the law . . . compromises dialogue between the two continents and possible negotiations between them."

Commentators were less reserved. Argentine political scientist Atilio Boron dismissed Europe as "the whore of Babylon," cringing before power.

With virtually identical reservations, two states refused

to sign the OAS resolution: the United States and Canada. Their growing isolation in the hemisphere as Latin America frees itself from the imperial yoke after 500 years is of historic significance.

Morales' plane, reporting technical problems, was permitted to land in Austria. Bolivia charges that the plane was searched to discover whether Snowden was on board. Austria responds that "there was no formal inspection." Whatever happened followed warnings delivered from Washington. Beyond that the story is murky.

Washington has made clear that any country that refuses to extradite Snowden will face harsh punishment. The United States will "chase him to the ends of the earth," Senator Lindsey Graham warned.

But U.S. government spokespersons assured the world that Snowden will be granted the full protection of American law—referring to those same laws that have kept U.S. Army soldier Bradley Manning (who released a vast archive of U.S. military and diplomatic documents to WikiLeaks) in prison for three years, much of it in solitary confinement under humiliating conditions. Long gone is the archaic notion of a speedy trial before a jury of peers. On July 30 a military judge found Manning guilty of charges that could lead to a maximum sentence of 136 years.

Like Snowden, Manning committed the crime of revealing to Americans—and others—what their government is doing. That is a severe breach of "security" in the operative meaning of the term, familiar to anyone who has pored over declassified documents. Typically "security" means security of government officials from the prying eyes of the public to whom they are answerable—in theory.

Governments always plead security as an excuse—in the

Snowden case, security from terrorist attack. This pretext comes from an administration carrying out a grand international terrorist campaign with drones and special operations forces that is generating potential terrorists at every step.

Their indignation knows no bounds at the thought that someone wanted by the United States should receive asylum in Bolivia, which has an extradition treaty with the United States. Oddly missing from the tumult is the fact that extradition works both ways—again, in theory.

Last September, the United States rejected Bolivia's 2008 petition to extradite former president Gonzalo Sánchez de Lozada—"Goni"—to face charges of genocide and crimes against humanity. It would, however, be an error to compare Bolivia's request for extradition with Washington's, even if we were to suppose that the cases have comparable merit.

The reason was provided by St. Augustine in his tale about the pirate asked by Alexander the Great, "How dare you molest the sea?" The pirate replied, "How dare you molest the whole world? Because I do it with a little ship only, I am called a thief; you, doing it with a great navy, are called an Emperor."

St. Augustine calls the pirate's answer "elegant and excellent." But the ancient philosopher, a bishop in Roman Africa, is only a voice from the global South, easily dismissed. Modern sophisticates comprehend that the Emperor has rights that little folk like Bolivians cannot aspire to.

Goni is only one of many that the Emperor chooses not to extradite. Another case is that of Luis Posada Carriles, described by Peter Kornbluh, an analyst of Latin American terror, as "one of the most dangerous terrorists in recent history."

Posada is wanted by Venezuela and Cuba for his role in the 1976 bombing of a Cubana commercial airliner, killing 73 people. The CIA and FBI identified him as a suspect. But Cubans and Venezuelans also lack the prerogatives of the Emperor, who organized and backed the reign of terror to which Cubans have been subjected since liberation.

The late Orlando Bosch, Posada's partner in terrorism, also benefited from the Emperor's benevolence. The Justice Department and FBI requested that he be deported as a threat to U.S. security, charging him with dozens of terrorist acts. In 1990, after President George H.W. Bush overturned the deportation order, Bosch lived the rest of his life happily in Miami, undisturbed by calls for extradition by Cuba and Costa Rica, two mere pirates.

Another insignificant pirate is Italy, now seeking the extradition of 23 CIA operatives indicted for kidnapping Hassan Mustafa Osama Nasr, an Egyptian cleric in Milan, whom they rendered to Egypt for torture (he was later found to be innocent). Good luck, Italy.

There are other cases, but the crime of rendition returns us to the matter of Latin American independence. The Open Society Institute recently released a study called "Globalizing Torture: CIA Secret Detention and Extraordinary Rendition." It reviewed global participation in the crime, which was very broad, including among European countries.

Latin American scholar Greg Grandin pointed out that one region was absent from the list of shame: Latin America. That is doubly remarkable. Latin America had long been the reliable "backyard" for the United States. If any of the locals sought to raise their heads, they would be decapitated by terror or military coup. And as it was under U.S. control throughout the latter half of the last century, Latin America was one of the torture capitals of the world.

That's no longer the case, as the United States and Canada are being virtually expelled from the hemisphere.

THE "HONEST BROKER" IS CROOKED
August 30, 2013

The Israel-Palestine negotiations currently under way in Jerusalem coincide with the 20th anniversary of the Oslo Accords. A look at the character of the accords and their fate may help explain the prevailing skepticism about the current exercise.

In September 1993, President Clinton presided over a handshake between Israeli Prime Minister Yitzhak Rabin and Palestine Liberation Organization (PLO) Chairman Yasser Arafat on the White House lawn—the climax of a "day of awe," as the press described it.

The occasion was the announcement of the Declaration of Principles for political settlement of the Israel-Palestine conflict, which resulted from secret meetings in Oslo that were sponsored by the Norwegian government.

Public negotiations between Israel and the Palestinians had opened in Madrid in November 1991, initiated by Washington in the triumphal glow after the first Iraq war. They were stalemated because the Palestinian delegation, led by the respected nationalist Haidar Abdul Shafi, insisted on ending Israel's expansion of its illegal settlements in the Occupied Territories.

In the immediate background were formal positions on the basic issues released by the PLO, Israel and the United States. In a November 1988 declaration, the PLO called for two states on the internationally recognized border, a proposal that the United States had vetoed at the Security Council in 1976 and continued to block, defying an overwhelming international consensus.

In May 1989 Israel responded, declaring that there can be no "additional Palestinian state" between Jordan and Israel (Jordan being a Palestinian state by Israeli dictate), and that further negotiations will be "in accordance with the basic guidelines of the [Israeli] Government." The Bush I administration endorsed this plan without qualifications, then initiated the Madrid negotiations as the "honest broker."

Then in 1993, the Declaration of Principles was quite explicit about satisfying Israel's demands but silent on Palestinian national rights. It conformed to the conception articulated by Dennis Ross, Clinton's main Middle East Advisor and negotiator at Camp David in 2000, later President Obama's main advisor as well. As Ross explained, Israel has needs but Palestinians only have wants, obviously of lesser significance.

Article I of the Declaration of Principles states that the end result of the process is to be "a permanent settlement based on Security Council Resolutions 242 and 338," which say nothing about Palestinian rights, apart from a vague reference to a "just settlement of the refugee problem."

If the "peace process" unfolded as the Declaration of Principles clearly stated, Palestinians could kiss goodbye their hopes for some limited degree of national rights in the Land of Israel.

Other Declaration of Principles articles stipulate that Palestinian authority extends over "West Bank and Gaza Strip territory, except for issues that will be negotiated in the permanent status negotiations: Jerusalem, settlements, military locations and Israelis"—that is, except for every issue of significance.

Furthermore, "Israel will continue to be responsible for external security, and for internal security and public order of settlements and Israelis. Israeli military forces and civilians may continue to use roads freely within the Gaza Strip and the Jericho area," the two areas from which Israel was pledged to withdraw—eventually.

In short, there would be no meaningful changes. The

Declaration of Principles also did not include a word about the settlement programs at the heart of the conflict: Even before the Oslo process, the settlements were undermining realistic prospects of achieving any meaningful Palestinian self-determination.

Only by succumbing to what is sometimes called "intentional ignorance" could one believe that the Oslo process was a path to peace. Nevertheless, this became virtual dogma among Western commentators.

As the Madrid negotiations opened, Danny Rubinstein, one of Israel's best-informed analysts, predicted that Israel and the United States would agree to some form of Palestinian "autonomy," but it would be "autonomy as in a POW camp, where the prisoners are 'autonomous' to cook their meals without interference and to organize cultural events." Rubenstein turned out to be correct.

The settlement programs continued after the Oslo Accords, at the same high level they had reached when Yitzhak Rabin became prime minister in 1992, extending well to the east of illegally annexed Greater Jerusalem.

As Rabin explained, Israel should take over "most of the territory of the Land of Israel [the former Palestine], whose capital is Jerusalem."

Meanwhile the United States and Israel moved to separate Gaza from the West Bank by closing access to it, in explicit violation of the terms of the accords, thus ensuring that any potential Palestinian entity would be cut off from the outside world.

The accords were followed by additional Israel-PLO agreements, which spelled out more clearly the terms of the autonomy of the POW camp. After Rabin's assassination, Shimon Peres became prime minister. As Peres left office in 1995, he assured the press that there would be no Palestinian state.

Norwegian scholar Hilde Henriksen Waage concluded that the "Oslo process could serve as the perfect case study for flaws" of the model of "third party mediation by a small state in highly asymmetrical conflicts. The question to be asked is whether such a model can ever be appropriate."

That question is well worth pondering, particularly as educated Western opinion now follows the ludicrous assumption that meaningful Israel-Palestine negotiations can be seriously conducted under the auspices of the United States—not an "honest broker," but in reality a partner of Israel.

As the current negotiations opened, Israel at once made its attitude clear by expanding the "National Priority List" for special subsidies to settlements scattered in the West Bank and by carrying forward its plans to build a train line to integrate the settlements more closely into Israel.

Obama followed suit by appointing as chief negotiator Martin Indyk, a close associate of Dennis Ross, whose background is as a lobbyist for Israel and who explains that Arabs are unable to comprehend the "idealism" and "generosity of spirit" that infuse all of Washington's efforts.

The negotiations provide a cover for Israel's takeover of the territories it wishes to control and should spare the United States some further embarrassment at the United Nations. That is, Palestine may agree to defer initiatives that would enhance its U.N. status—which the U.S. would be compelled to block, joined by Israel and perhaps Palau.

It is, however, unlikely that the negotiations will advance the prospects for a meaningful peace settlement.

THE OBAMA DOCTRINE

October 4, 2013

The recent Obama-Putin tiff over American exceptionalism reignited an ongoing debate over the Obama Doctrine: Is the president veering toward isolationism? Or will he proudly carry the banner of exceptionalism?

The debate is narrower that it may seem. There is considerable common ground between the two positions, as was expressed clearly by Hans Morgenthau, the founder of the now dominant no-sentimentality "realist" school of international relations.

Throughout his work, Morgenthau describes America as unique among all powers past and present in that it has a "transcendent purpose" that it "must defend and promote" throughout the world: "the establishment of equality in freedom."

The competing concepts "exceptionalism" and "isolationism" both accept this doctrine and its various elaborations but differ with regard to its application.

One extreme was vigorously defended by President Obama in his September 10 address to the nation: "What makes America different," he declared, "what makes us exceptional," is that we are dedicated to act, "with humility, but with resolve," when we detect violations somewhere.

"For nearly seven decades the United States has been the anchor of global security," a role that "has meant more than forging international agreements; it has meant enforcing them."

The competing doctrine, isolationism, holds that we can no longer afford to carry out the noble mission of racing to put out the fires lit by others. It takes seriously a cautionary note sounded 20 years ago by the *NEW YORK TIMES* columnist Thomas Friedman that "granting idealism a near exclusive hold on our foreign policy" may lead us to neglect our own interests in our devotion to the needs of others.

Between these extremes, the debate over foreign policy rages.

At the fringes, some observers reject the shared assumptions, bringing up the historical record: for example, the fact that "for nearly seven decades" the United States has led the world in aggression and subversion—overthrowing elected governments and imposing vicious dictatorships, supporting horrendous crimes, undermining international agreements and leaving trails of blood, destruction and misery.

To these misguided creatures, Morgenthau provided an answer. A serious scholar, he recognized that America has consistently violated its "transcendent purpose."

But to bring up this objection, he explains, is to commit "the error of atheism, which denies the validity of religion on similar grounds." It is the transcendent purpose of America that is "reality"; the actual historical record is merely "the abuse of reality."

In short, "American exceptionalism" and "isolationism" are generally understood to be tactical variants of a secular religion, with a grip that is quite extraordinary, going beyond normal religious orthodoxy in that it can barely even be perceived. Since no alternative is thinkable, this faith is adopted reflexively.

Others express the doctrine more crudely. One of President Reagan's U.N. ambassadors, Jeane Kirkpatrick, devised a new method to deflect criticism of state crimes. Those unwilling to dismiss them as mere "blunders" or "innocent naïveté" can be charged with "moral equivalence"—of claiming that the United States is no different from Nazi Germany, or whoever the current demon may be. The device has since been widely used to protect power from scrutiny.

Even serious scholarship conforms. Thus in the current issue of the journal DIPLOMATIC HISTORY, scholar Jeffrey A. Engel reflects on the significance of history for policy makers.

Engel cites Vietnam, where, "depending on one's political persuasion," the lesson is either "avoidance of the quick-sand of escalating intervention [isolationism] or the need to provide military commanders free rein to operate devoid of political pressure"—as we carried out our mission to bring stability, equality and freedom by destroying three countries and leaving millions of corpses.

The Vietnam death toll continues to mount into the present because of the chemical warfare that President Kennedy initiated there—even as he escalated American support for a murderous dictatorship to all-out attack, the worst case of aggression during Obama's "seven decades."

Another "political persuasion" is imaginable: the outrage Americans adopt when Russia invades Afghanistan or Saddam Hussein invades Kuwait. But the secular religion bars us from seeing ourselves through a similar lens.

One mechanism of self-protection is to lament the consequences of our failure to act. Thus NEW YORK TIMES columnist David Brooks, ruminating on the drift of Syria to "Rwanda-like" horror, concludes that the deeper issue is the Sunni-Shiite violence tearing the region asunder.

That violence is a testimony to the failure "of the recent American strategy of light-footprint withdrawal" and the loss of what former foreign service officer Gary Grappo calls the "moderating influence of American forces."

Those still deluded by "abuse of reality"—that is, fact—might recall that the Sunni-Shiite violence resulted from the worst crime of aggression of the new millennium, the U.S. invasion of Iraq. And those burdened with richer memories might recall that the Nuremberg Trials sentenced Nazi criminals to hanging because, according to the Tribunal's judgment, aggression is "the supreme international crime differing only from other war crimes in that it contains within itself the accumulated evil of the whole."

The same lament is the topic of a celebrated study by Samantha Power, the new U.S. ambassador to the United Nations. In *A PROBLEM FROM HELL: AMERICA IN THE AGE OF GENOCIDE*, Power writes about the crimes of others and our inadequate response.

She devotes a sentence to one of the few cases during the seven decades that might truly rank as genocide: the Indonesian invasion of East Timor in 1975. Tragically, the United States "looked away," Power reports.

Daniel Patrick Moynihan, her predecessor as U.N. ambassador at the time of the invasion, saw the matter differently. In his book *A DANGEROUS PLACE*, he described with great pride how he rendered the United Nations "utterly ineffective in whatever measures it undertook" to end the aggression, because "the United States wished things to turn out as they did."

And indeed, far from looking away, Washington gave a green light to the Indonesian invaders and immediately provided them with lethal military equipment. The U.S. prevented the U.N. Security Council from acting and continued to lend firm support to the aggressors and their genocidal actions, including the atrocities of 1999, until President Clinton called a halt—as could have happened anytime during the previous 25 years.

But that is mere abuse of reality.

It is all too easy to continue, but also pointless. Brooks is right to insist that we should go beyond the terrible events before our eyes and reflect about the deeper processes and their lessons.

Among these, no task is more urgent than to free ourselves from the religious doctrines that consign the actual events of history to oblivion and thereby reinforce our basis for further "abuses of reality."

DE-AMERICANIZING THE WORLD

November 4, 2013

During the latest episode of the Washington farce that has astonished a bemused world, a Chinese commentator wrote that if the United States cannot be a responsible member of the world system, perhaps the world should become "de-Americanized"—and separate itself from the rogue state that is the reigning military power but is losing credibility in other domains.

The Washington debacle's immediate source was the sharp shift to the right among the political class. In the past, the U.S. has sometimes been described sardonically—but not inaccurately—as a one-party state: the business party, with two factions called Democrats and Republicans.

That is no longer true. The U.S. is still a one-party state, the business party. But it only has one faction: moderate Republicans, now called New Democrats (as the U.S. Congressional coalition styles itself).

There is still a Republican organization, but it long ago abandoned any pretense of being a normal parliamentary party. Conservative commentator Norman Ornstein of the American Enterprise Institute describes today's Republicans as "a radical insurgency—ideologically extreme, scornful of facts and compromise, dismissive of the legitimacy of its political opposition": a serious danger to society.

The party is in lock-step service to the very rich and the corporate sector. Since votes cannot be obtained on that platform, the party has been compelled to mobilize sectors of the society that are extremist by world standards. Crazy is the new norm among Tea Party members and a host of others beyond the mainstream.

The Republican establishment and its business sponsors

had expected to use them as a battering ram in the neoliberal assault against the population—to privatize, to deregulate and to limit government, while retaining those parts that serve wealth and power, like the military.

The Republican establishment has had some success, but now finds that it can no longer control its base, much to its dismay. The impact on American society thus becomes even more severe. A case in point: the virulent reaction against the Affordable Care Act and the near-shutdown of the government.

The Chinese commentator's observation is not entirely novel. In 1999, political analyst Samuel P. Huntington warned that for much of the world, the United States is "becoming the rogue superpower," seen as "the single greatest external threat to their societies."

A few months into the Bush term, Robert Jervis, president of the American Political Science Association, warned that "in the eyes of much of the world, in fact, the prime rogue state today is the United States." Both Huntington and Jervis warned that such a course is unwise. The consequences for the United States could be harmful.

In the latest issue of *FOREIGN AFFAIRS*, the leading establishment journal, David Kaye reviews one aspect of Washington's departure from the world: rejection of multilateral treaties "as if it were sport."

He explains that some treaties are rejected outright, as when the U.S. Senate "voted against the Convention on the Rights of Persons with Disabilities in 2012 and the Comprehensive Nuclear-Test-Ban Treaty (CTBT) in 1999."

Others are dismissed by inaction, including "such subjects as labor, economic and cultural rights, endangered species, pollution, armed conflict, peacekeeping, nuclear weapons, the law of the sea, and discrimination against women."

Rejection of international obligations "has grown so entrenched," Kaye writes, "that foreign governments no longer expect Washington's ratification or its full participation in the institutions treaties create. The world is moving on; laws get made elsewhere, with limited (if any) American involvement."

While not new, the practice has indeed become more entrenched in recent years, along with quiet acceptance at home of the doctrine that the United States has every right to act as a rogue state.

To take a typical example, a few weeks ago U.S. special operations forces snatched a suspect, Abu Anas al-Libi, from the streets of the Libyan capital, Tripoli, bringing him to a naval vessel for interrogation without counsel or rights. U.S. Secretary of State John Kerry informed the press that the actions are legal because they comply with American law, eliciting no particular comment.

Principles are valid only if they are universal. Reactions would be a bit different, needless to say, if Cuban special forces kidnapped the prominent terrorist Luis Posada Carriles in Miami, bringing him to Cuba for interrogation and trial in accordance with Cuban law.

Such actions are restricted to rogue states. More accurately, to the one rogue state that is powerful enough to act with impunity: in recent years, to carry out aggression at will, to terrorize large regions of the world with drone attacks, and much else.

And to defy the world in other ways, for example by persisting in its embargo against Cuba despite the long-term opposition of the entire world, apart from Israel, which voted with its protector when the United Nations again condemned the embargo (188-2) in October.

Whatever the world may think, U.S. actions are legitimate because we say so. The principle was enunciated by the

eminent statesman Dean Acheson in 1962, when he instructed the American Society of International Law that no legal
issue arises when the United States responds to a challenge to
its "power, position, and prestige."

Cuba committed that crime when it beat back a U.S. invasion and then had the audacity to survive an assault designed
to bring "the terrors of the earth" to Cuba, in the words of
Kennedy adviser and historian Arthur Schlesinger.

When the United States gained independence, it sought
to join the international community of the day. That is why
the Declaration of Independence opens by expressing concern for the "decent respect to the opinions of mankind."

A crucial element was evolution from a disorderly con-
federacy to a unified "treaty-worthy nation," in diplomatic
historian Eliga H. Gould's phrase, that observed the conven-
tions of the European order. By achieving this status, the new
nation also gained the right to act as it wished internally.

It could thus proceed to rid itself of the indigenous population and to expand slavery, an institution so "odious" that it
could not be tolerated in England, as the distinguished jurist
William Murray, Earl of Mansfield, ruled in 1772. Evolving
English law was a factor impelling the slave-owning society
to escape its reach.

Becoming a treaty-worthy nation thus conferred multiple advantages: foreign recognition, and the freedom to act at
home without interference. Hegemonic power offers the opportunity to become a rogue state, freely defying international
law and norms, while facing increased resistance abroad and
contributing to its own decline through self-inflicted wounds.

THE "AXIS OF EVIL," REVISITED

December 3, 2013

An interim agreement on Iran's nuclear policies that will provide a six-month period for substantive negotiations was announced on November 24.

Michael Gordon, a reporter for the *NEW YORK TIMES*, wrote, "It was the first time in nearly a decade, American officials said, that an international agreement had been reached to halt much of Iran's nuclear program and roll some elements of it back."

The United States moved at once to impose severe penalties on a Swiss firm that had violated U.S.-imposed sanctions. "The timing of the announcement seemed to be partly intended to send a signal that the Obama administration still considers Iran subject to economic isolation," Rick Gladstone explained in the *TIMES*.

The "landmark accord" indeed includes significant Iranian concessions—though nothing comparable from the United States, which merely agreed to temporarily limit its punishment of Iran.

It's easy to imagine possible U.S. concessions. To mention just one: The United States is the only country directly violating the Nuclear Non-Proliferation Treaty (NPT)—and more severely, the United Nations Charter—by maintaining its threat of force against Iran. The United States could also insist that its Israeli client refrain from this severe violation of international law—which is just one of many.

In mainstream discourse, it is considered natural that Iran alone should make concessions. After all, the United States is the White Knight, leading the international community in its efforts to contain Iran—which is held to be the gravest threat to world peace—and to compel it to refrain from its aggression, terror and other crimes.

There is a different perspective, little heard, though it might be worth at least a mention. It begins by rejecting the American assertion that the accord breaks 10 years of unwillingness on Iran's part to address this alleged nuclear threat.

Ten years ago Iran offered to resolve its differences with the United States over nuclear programs, along with all other issues. The Bush administration rejected the offer angrily and reprimanded the Swiss diplomat who conveyed it.

The European Union and Iran then sought an arrangement under which Iran would suspend uranium enrichment while the EU would provide assurances that the U.S. would not attack. As Selig Harrison reported in the *FINANCIAL TIMES*, "the EU, held back by the U.S. . . . refused to discuss security issues," and the effort died.

In 2010, Iran accepted a proposal by Turkey and Brazil to ship its enriched uranium to Turkey for storage. In return, the West would provide isotopes for Iran's medical research reactors. President Obama furiously denounced Brazil and Turkey for breaking ranks, and quickly imposed harsher sanctions. Irritated, Brazil released a letter from Obama in which he had proposed this arrangement, presumably assuming that Iran would reject it. The incident quickly disappeared from view.

Also in 2010, the NPT members called for an international conference to carry forward a long-standing Arab initiative to establish a zone free of weapons of mass destruction in the region, to be held in Helsinki in December 2012. Israel refused to attend. Iran agreed to do so, unconditionally.

The United States then announced that the conference was canceled, reiterating Israel's objections. The Arab states, the European Parliament and Russia called for a rapid reconvening of the conference, while the U.N. General Assembly voted 174-6 to call on Israel to join the NPT and open its facilities to inspection. Voting "no" were the United States, Israel, Canada, Marshall Islands, Micronesia and Palau—a result that suggests another possible U.S. concession today.

Such isolation of the United States in the international arena is quite normal, on a wide range of issues.

In contrast, the Non-Aligned Movement (most of the world), at its meeting last year in Tehran, once again vigorously supported Iran's right, as a signer of the NPT, to enrich uranium. The U.S. rejects that argument, claiming that the right is conditional on a clean bill of health from inspectors, but there is no such wording in the treaty.

A large majority of Arabs support Iran's right to pursue its nuclear program. Arabs are hostile to Iran, but overwhelmingly regard the United States and Israel as the primary threats they face, as Shibley Telhami reported again in his recent comprehensive review of Arab opinion.

"Western officials appear flummoxed" by Iran's refusal to abandon the right to enrich uranium, Frank Rose observes in the *NEW YORK TIMES*, offering a psychological explanation. Others come to mind if we step slightly out of the box.

The United States can be held to lead the international community only if that community is defined as the United States and whoever happens to go along with it, often through intimidation, as is sometimes tacitly conceded.

Critics of the new accord, as David E. Sanger and Jodi Rudoren report in the *NEW YORK TIMES*, warn that "wily middlemen, Chinese eager for energy sources and Europeans looking for a way back to the old days, when Iran was a major source of trade, will see their chance to leap the barriers." In short, they currently accept American orders only because of fear. And in fact China, India and many others have sought their own ways to evade U.S. sanctions on Iran.

The alternative perspective challenges the rest of the standard U.S. version. It does not overlook the fact that for 60 years, without a break, the United States has been torturing Iranians. That punishment began in 1953 with the CIA-run coup that overthrew Iran's parliamentary government and installed the Shah, a tyrant who regularly compiled one of the worst human rights records in the world as an American ally.

When the Shah was himself overthrown in 1979, the U.S. turned at once to supporting Saddam Hussein's murderous invasion of Iran, finally joining directly by reflagging Iraq ally Kuwait's ships so that they could break an Iranian blockade. In 1988 a U.S. naval vessel also shot down an Iranian airliner in commercial airspace, killing 290 people, then received presidential honors upon returning home.

After Iran was forced to capitulate, the United States renewed its support for its friend Saddam, even inviting Iraqi nuclear engineers to the U.S. for advanced training in weapons production. The Clinton administration then imposed sanctions on Iran, which have become much harsher in recent years.

There are in fact two rogue states operating in the region, resorting to aggression and terror and violating international law at will: the United States and its Israeli client. Iran has indeed carried out an act of aggression: conquering three Arab islands under the U.S.-backed Shah. But any terror credibly attributed to Iran pales in comparison with that of the rogue states.

It is understandable that those rogue states should strenuously object to a deterrent in the region, and should lead a campaign to free themselves from any such constraints.

Just how far will the lesser rogue state go to eliminate the feared deterrent on the pretext of an "existential threat"? Some fear that it will go very far. Micah Zenko of the Council on Foreign Relations warns in FOREIGN POLICY that Israel might resort to nuclear war. Foreign policy analyst Zbigniew Brzezinski urges Washington to make it clear to Israel that the U.S. Air Force will stop them if they try to bomb.

Which of these conflicting perspectives is closer to reality? To answer the question is more than just a useful exercise. Significant global consequences turn on the answer.

WHAT IS THE COMMON GOOD?

January 6, 2014

THIS ARTICLE IS ADAPTED FROM A DEWEY LECTURE BY
NOAM CHOMSKY AT COLUMBIA UNIVERSITY IN NEW YORK
ON DECEMBER 6, 2013.

Humans are social beings, and the kind of creature that a person becomes depends crucially on the social, cultural and institutional circumstances of his or her life.

We are therefore led to inquire into the social arrangements that are conducive to people's rights and welfare, and to fulfilling their just aspirations—in brief, the common good.

For perspective I'd like to invoke what seem to me virtual truisms. They relate to an interesting category of ethical principles: those that are not only universal, in that they are virtually always professed, but also doubly universal, in that at the same time they are almost universally rejected in practice.

These range from very general principles, such as the truism that we should apply to ourselves the same standards we do to others (if not harsher ones), to more specific doctrines, such as a dedication to promoting democracy and human rights, which is proclaimed almost universally, even by the worst monsters—though the actual record is grim, across the spectrum.

A good place to start is with John Stuart Mill's classic *ON LIBERTY*. Its epigraph formulates "The grand, leading principle, towards which every argument unfolded in these pages directly converges: the absolute and essential importance of human development in its richest diversity."

The words are quoted from Wilhelm von Humboldt, a founder of classical liberalism. It follows that institutions that constrain such development are illegitimate, unless they can somehow justify themselves.

Concern for the common good should impel us to find ways to cultivate human development in its richest diversity.

Adam Smith, another Enlightenment thinker with similar views, felt that it shouldn't be too difficult to institute humane policies. In his *THEORY OF MORAL SENTIMENTS* he observed that "How selfish soever man may be supposed, there are evidently some principles in his nature, which interest him in the fortune of others, and render their happiness necessary to him, though he derives nothing from it except the pleasure of seeing it."

Smith acknowledges the power of what he calls the "vile maxim of the masters of mankind": "All for ourselves, and nothing for other people." But the more benign "original passions of human nature" might compensate for that pathology.

Classical liberalism shipwrecked on the shoals of capitalism, but its humanistic commitments and aspirations didn't die. Rudolf Rocker, a 20th-century anarchist thinker and activist, reiterated similar ideas.

Rocker described what he calls "a definite trend in the historic development of mankind" that strives for "the free unhindered unfolding of all the individual and social forces in life."

Rocker was outlining an anarchist tradition culminating in anarcho-syndicalism—in European terms, a variety of "libertarian socialism."

This brand of socialism, he held, doesn't depict "a fixed, self-enclosed social system" with a definite answer to all the multifarious questions and problems of human life, but rather a trend in human development that strives to attain Enlightenment ideals.

So understood, anarchism is part of a broader range of

libertarian socialist thought and action that includes the practical achievements of revolutionary Spain in 1936; reaches further to worker-owned enterprises spreading today in the American rust belt, in northern Mexico, in Egypt, and many other countries, most extensively in the Basque country in Spain; and encompasses the many cooperative movements around the world and a good part of feminist and civil and human-rights initiatives.

This broad tendency in human development seeks to identify structures of hierarchy, authority and domination that constrain human development, and then subject them to a very reasonable challenge: Justify yourself.

If these structures can't meet that challenge, they should be dismantled—and, anarchists believe, "refashioned from below," as commentator Nathan Schneider observes.

In part this sounds like truism: Why should anyone defend illegitimate structures and institutions? But truisms at least have the merit of being true, which distinguishes them from a good deal of political discourse. And I think they provide useful stepping stones to finding the common good.

For Rocker, "the problem that is set for our time is that of freeing man from the curse of economic exploitation and political and social enslavement."

It should be noted that the American brand of libertarianism differs sharply from the libertarian tradition, accepting and indeed advocating the subordination of working people to the masters of the economy, and the subjection of everyone to the restrictive discipline and destructive features of markets.

Anarchism is, famously, opposed to the state, while advocating "planned administration of things in the interest of the community," in Rocker's words; and beyond that, wide-ranging federations of self-governing communities and workplaces.

Today, anarchists dedicated to these goals often support state power to protect people, society and the earth itself from the ravages of concentrated private capital. That's no contradiction. People live and suffer and endure in the existing society. Available means should be used to safeguard and benefit them, even if a long-term goal is to construct preferable alternatives.

In the Brazilian rural workers movement, they speak of "widening the floors of the cage"—the cage of existing coercive institutions that can be widened by popular struggle—as has happened effectively over many years.

We can extend the image to think of the cage of state institutions as a protection from the savage beasts roaming outside: the predatory, state-supported capitalist institutions dedicated in principle to private gain, power and domination, with community and people's interest at most a footnote, revered in rhetoric but dismissed in practice as a matter of principle and even law.

Much of the most respected work in academic political science compares public attitudes and government policy. In *AFFLUENCE AND INFLUENCE: ECONOMIC INEQUALITY AND POLITICAL POWER IN AMERICA*, the Princeton scholar Martin Gilens reveals that the majority of the U.S. population is effectively disenfranchised.

About 70 percent of the population, at the lower end of the wealth/income scale, has no influence on policy, Gilens concludes. Moving up the scale, influence slowly increases. At the very top are those who pretty much determine policy, by means that aren't obscure. The resulting system is not democracy but plutocracy.

Or perhaps, a little more kindly, it's what legal scholar Conor Gearty calls "neo-democracy," a partner to neoliberalism—a system in which liberty is enjoyed by the few, and security in its fullest sense is available only to the elite, but within a system of more general formal rights.

In contrast, as Rocker writes, a truly democratic system would achieve the character of "an alliance of free groups of men and women based on cooperative labor and a planned administration of things in the interest of the community."

No one took the American philosopher John Dewey to be an anarchist. But consider his ideas. He recognized that "power today resides in control of the means of production, exchange, publicity, transportation and communication. Whoever owns them rules the life of the country," even if democratic forms remain. Until those institutions are in the hands of the public, politics will remain "the shadow cast on society by big business," much as is seen today.

These ideas lead very naturally to a vision of society based on workers' control of productive institutions, as envisioned by 19th-century thinkers, notably Karl Marx but also—less familiar—John Stuart Mill.

Mill wrote, "The form of association, however, which if mankind continue to improve, must be expected to predominate, is . . . the association of the labourers themselves on terms of equality, collectively owning the capital with which they carry on their operations, and working under managers electable and removable by themselves."

The Founding Fathers of the United States were well aware of the hazards of democracy. In the Constitutional Convention debates, the main framer, James Madison, warned of these hazards.

Naturally taking England as his model, Madison observed that "in England, at this day, if elections were open to all classes of people, the property of landed proprietors would be insecure. An agrarian law would soon take place," undermining the right to property.

The basic problem that Madison foresaw in "framing a system which we wish to last for ages" was to ensure that the actual rulers will be the wealthy minority so as "to secure the rights of property agst. the danger from an equality & universality of suffrage, vesting compleat power over property in hands without a share in it."

Scholarship generally agrees with the Brown University scholar Gordon S. Wood's assessment that "the Constitution was intrinsically an aristocratic document designed to check the democratic tendencies of the period."

Long before Madison, Artistotle, in his *POLITICS*, recognized the same problem with democracy.

Reviewing a variety of political systems, Aristotle concluded that this system was the best—or perhaps the least bad—form of government. But he recognized a flaw: The great mass of the poor could use their voting power to take the property of the rich, which would be unfair.

Madison and Aristotle arrived at opposite solutions: Aristotle advised reducing inequality, by what we would regard as welfare state measures. Madison felt that the answer was to reduce democracy.

In his last years, Thomas Jefferson, the man who drafted the United States' Declaration of Independence, captured the essential nature of the conflict, which has far from ended. Jefferson had serious concerns about the quality and fate of the democratic experiment. He distinguished between "aristocrats and democrats."

The aristocrats are "those who fear and distrust the people, and wish to draw all powers from them into the hands of the higher classes."

The democrats, in contrast, "identify with the people, have confidence in them, cherish and consider them as the most honest and safe, although not the most wise depository of the public interest."

Today the successors to Jefferson's "aristocrats" might argue about who should play the guiding role: technocratic and policy-oriented intellectuals, or bankers and corporate executives.

It is this political guardianship that the genuine libertarian tradition seeks to dismantle and reconstruct from below, while also changing industry, as Dewey put it, "from a feudalistic to a democratic social order" based on workers' control, respecting the dignity of the producer as a genuine person, not a tool in the hands of others.

Like Karl Marx's Old Mole—"our old friend, our old mole, who knows so well how to work underground, then suddenly to emerge"—the libertarian tradition is always burrowing close to the surface, always ready to peek through, sometimes in surprising and unexpected ways, seeking to bring about what seems to me to be a reasonable approximation to the common good.

PREROGATIVES OF POWER
February 4, 2014

As the year 2013 drew to an end, the BBC reported on the results of the WIN/Gallup International poll on the question: "Which country do you think is the greatest threat to peace in the world today?"

The United States was the champion by a substantial margin, winning three times the votes of second-place Pakistan.

By contrast, the debate in American scholarly and media circles is about whether Iran can be contained, and whether the huge NSA surveillance system is needed to protect U.S. security.

In view of the poll, it would seem that there are more pertinent questions: Can the United States be contained and other nations secured in the face of the U.S. threat?

In some parts of the world the United States ranks even higher as a perceived menace to world peace, notably in the Middle East, where overwhelming majorities regard the U.S. and its close ally Israel as the major threats they face, not the U.S.-Israeli favorite: Iran.

Few Latin Americans are likely to question the judgment of Cuban nationalist hero José Martí, who wrote in 1894, "The further they draw away from the United States, the freer and more prosperous the [Latin] American people will be."

Martí's judgment has been well-confirmed in recent years, once again by the analysis of poverty by the U.N. Economic Commission for Latin America and the Caribbean, released last month.

The U.N. report shows that far-reaching reforms have sharply reduced poverty in Brazil, Uruguay, Venezuela and some other countries where U.S. influence is slight, but that it remains abysmal in others—namely, those that have long been under U.S. domination, like Guatemala and Honduras. Even in relatively wealthy Mexico, under the umbrella of the North American Free Trade Agreement, poverty is severe, with 1 million added to the numbers of the poor in 2013.

Sometimes the reasons for the world's concerns are obliquely recognized in the United States, as when former CIA director Michael Hayden, discussing Obama's drone murder campaign, conceded that "right now, there isn't a government on the planet that agrees with our legal rationale for these operations, except for Afghanistan and maybe Israel."

A normal country would be concerned by how it is viewed in the world. Certainly that would be true of a country committed to "a decent respect to the opinions of mankind," to quote the Founding Fathers. But the United States is far from a normal country. It has been the most powerful economy in the world for a century, and has had no real challenge to its global hegemony since World War II, despite some decline, partly self-administered.

The United States, conscious of "soft power," undertakes major campaigns of "public diplomacy" (aka propaganda) to create a favorable image, sometimes accompanied by worthwhile policies that are welcomed. But when the world persists in believing that the United States is by far the greatest threat to peace, the American press scarcely reports the fact.

The ability to ignore unwanted facts is one of the prerogatives of unchallenged power. Closely related is the right to radically revise history.

A current example is the laments about the escalating Sunni-Shiite conflict that is tearing apart the Middle East, particularly in Iraq and Syria. The prevailing theme of U.S. commentary is that this strife is the terrible consequence of the withdrawal of American force from the region—a lesson in the dangers of "isolationism."

The opposite is more nearly correct. The roots of the conflict within Islam are many and varied, but it cannot be seriously denied that the split was significantly exacerbated by the American- and British-led invasion of Iraq. And it cannot be too often repeated that aggression was defined at the Nuremberg Trials as "the supreme international crime," differing from others in that it encompasses all the evil that follows, including the current catastrophe.

A remarkable illustration of this rapid inversion of history is the American reaction to the current atrocities in Fallujah. The dominant theme is the pain about the sacrifices, in vain, of the American soldiers who fought and died to liberate Fallujah. A look at the news reports of the U.S. assaults on Fallujah in 2004 quickly reveals that these were among the most vicious and disgraceful war crimes of that aggression.

The death of Nelson Mandela provides another occasion for reflection on the remarkable impact of what has been called "historical engineering": reshaping the facts of history to serve the needs of power.

When Mandela at last obtained his freedom, he declared that "during all my years in prison, Cuba was an inspiration and Fidel Castro a tower of strength. . . . [Cuban victories] destroyed the myth of the invincibility of the white oppressor [and] inspired the fighting masses of South Africa . . . a turning point for the liberation of our continent—and of my people—from the scourge of apartheid. . . . What other country can point to a record of greater selflessness than Cuba has displayed in its relations to Africa?"

Today the names of Cubans who died defending Angola from U.S.-backed South African aggression, defying American demands that they leave the country, are inscribed on the

"Wall of Names" in Pretoria's Freedom Park. And the thousands of Cuban aid workers who sustained Angola, largely at Cuban expense, are also not forgotten.

The U.S.-approved version is quite different. From the first days after South Africa's agreement to withdraw from illegally occupied Namibia in 1988, paving the way for the end of apartheid, the outcome was hailed by the *WALL STREET JOURNAL* as a "splendid achievement" of American diplomacy, "one of the most significant foreign policy achievements of the Reagan administration."

The reasons why Mandela and South Africans perceive a radically different picture are spelled out in Piero Gleijeses's masterful scholarly inquiry *VISIONS OF FREEDOM: HAVANA, WASHINGTON, PRETORIA, AND THE STRUGGLE FOR SOUTHERN AFRICA, 1976–1991.*

As Gleijeses convincingly demonstrates, South Africa's aggression and terrorism in Angola and its occupation of Namibia were ended by "Cuban military might" accompanied by "fierce black resistance" within South Africa and the courage of Namibian guerrillas. The Namibian liberation forces easily won fair elections as soon as these were possible. Similarly, in elections in Angola, the Cuban-backed government prevailed—while the United States continued to support vicious opposition terrorists there even after South Africa was compelled to back away.

To the end, the Reaganites remained virtually alone in their strong support for the apartheid regime and its murderous depredations in neighboring countries. Though these shameful episodes may be wiped out of internal U.S. history, others are likely to understand Mandela's words.

In these and all too many other cases, supreme power does provide protection against reality—to a point.

SECURITY AND STATE POLICY

March 3, 2014

THIS ARTICLE, THE FIRST OF TWO PARTS, IS ADAPTED FROM A LECTURE BY NOAM CHOMSKY ON FEBRUARY 28, SPONSORED BY THE NUCLEAR AGE PEACE FOUNDATION IN SANTA BARBARA, CALIFORNIA.

A leading principle of international relations theory is that the state's highest priority is to ensure security. As Cold War strategist George F. Kennan formulated the standard view, government is created "to assure order and justice internally and to provide for the common defense."

The proposition seems plausible, almost self-evident, until we look more closely and ask: Security for whom? For the general population? For state power itself? For dominant domestic constituencies?

Depending on what we mean, the credibility of the proposition ranges from negligible to very high.

Security for state power is at the high extreme, as illustrated by the efforts that states exert to protect themselves from the scrutiny of their own populations.

In an interview on German TV, Edward J. Snowden said that his "breaking point" was "seeing Director of National Intelligence, James Clapper, directly lie under oath to Congress" by denying the existence of a domestic spying program conducted by the National Security Agency.

Snowden elaborated that "the public had a right to know about these programs. The public had a right to know that which the government is doing in its name, and that which the government is doing against the public."

The same could be justly said by Daniel Ellsberg,

Chelsea Manning and other courageous figures who acted on the same democratic principle.

The government stance is quite different: The public doesn't have the right to know because security thus is undermined—severely so, as officials assert.

There are several good reasons to be skeptical about such a response. The first is that it's almost completely predictable: When a government's act is exposed, the government reflexively pleads security. The predictable response therefore carries little information.

A second reason for skepticism is the nature of the evidence presented. International relations scholar John Mearsheimer writes, "The Obama administration, not surprisingly, initially claimed that the NSA's spying played a key role in thwarting 54 terrorist plots against the United States, implying it violated the Fourth Amendment for good reason.

"This was a lie, however. General Keith Alexander, the NSA director, eventually admitted to Congress that he could claim only one success, and that involved catching a Somali immigrant and three cohorts living in San Diego who had sent $8,500 to a terrorist group in Somalia."

A similar conclusion was reached by the Privacy and Civil Liberties Oversight Board, established by the government to investigate the NSA programs and therefore granted extensive access to classified materials and to security officials.

There is, of course, a sense in which security is threatened by public awareness—namely, security of state power from exposure.

The basic insight was expressed well by the Harvard political scientist Samuel P. Huntington: "The architects of power in the United States must create a force that can be felt but not seen. Power remains strong when it remains in the dark; exposed to the sunlight it begins to evaporate."

In the United States as elsewhere, the architects of power understand that very well. Those who have worked through the huge mass of declassified documents in, for example, the official State Department history "Foreign Relations of the United States," can hardly fail to notice how frequently it is security of state power from the domestic public that is a prime concern, not national security in any meaningful sense.

Often the attempt to maintain secrecy is motivated by the need to guarantee the security of powerful domestic sectors. One persistent example is the mislabeled "free trade agreements"—mislabeled because they radically violate free trade principles and are substantially not about trade at all, but rather about investor rights.

These instruments are regularly negotiated in secret, like the current Trans-Pacific Partnership—not entirely in secret, of course. They aren't secret from the hundreds of corporate lobbyists and lawyers who are writing the detailed provisions, with an impact revealed by the few parts that have reached the public through WikiLeaks.

As the economist Joseph E. Stiglitz reasonably concludes, with the U.S. Trade Representative's office "representing corporate interests," not those of the public, "The likelihood that what emerges from the coming talks will serve ordinary Americans' interests is low; the outlook for ordinary citizens in other countries is even bleaker."

Corporate-sector security is a regular concern of government policies—which is hardly surprising, given their role in formulating the policies in the first place.

In contrast, there is substantial evidence that the security of the domestic population—"national security" as the term is supposed to be understood—is not a high priority for state policy.

For example, President Obama's drone-driven global assassination program, by far the world's greatest terrorist campaign, is also a terror-generating campaign. General Stanley A. McChrystal, commander of U.S. and NATO forces in Afghanistan until he was relieved of duty, spoke of "insurgent math": For every innocent person you kill, you create 10 new enemies.

This concept of "innocent person" tells us how far we've progressed in the last 800 years, since the Magna Carta, which established the principle of presumption of innocence that was once thought to be the foundation of Anglo-American law.

Today, the word "guilty" means "targeted for assassination by Obama," and "innocent" means "not yet accorded that status."

The Brookings Institution just published *THE THISTLE AND THE DRONE*, a highly praised anthropological study of tribal societies by Akbar Ahmed, subtitled *HOW AMERICA'S WAR ON TERROR BECAME A GLOBAL WAR ON TRIBAL ISLAM*.

This global war pressures repressive central governments to undertake assaults against Washington's tribal enemies. The war, Ahmed warns, may drive some tribes "to extinction"—with severe costs to the societies themselves, as seen now in Afghanistan, Pakistan, Somalia and Yemen. And ultimately to Americans.

Tribal cultures, Ahmed points out, are based on honor and revenge: "Every act of violence in these tribal societies provokes a counterattack: the harder the attacks on the tribesmen, the more vicious and bloody the counterattacks."

The terror targeting may hit home. In the British journal *INTERNATIONAL AFFAIRS*, David Hastings Dunn outlines how increasingly sophisticated drones are a perfect weapon for terrorist groups. Drones are cheap, easily acquired and "possess many qualities which, when combined, make them potentially the ideal means for terrorist attack in the 21st century," Dunn explains.

Senator Adlai Stevenson III, referring to his many years of service on the U.S. Senate Intelligence Committee, writes that "cyber surveillance and meta data collection are part of the continuing reaction to 9/11, with few if any terrorists to show for it and near universal condemnation. The U.S. is widely perceived as waging war against Islam, against Shiites as well as Sunnis, on the ground, with drones, and by proxy in Palestine, from the Persian Gulf to Central Asia. Germany and Brazil resent our intrusions, and what have they wrought?"

The answer is that they have wrought a growing terror threat as well as international isolation.

The drone assassination campaigns are one device by which state policy knowingly endangers security. The same is true of murderous special-forces operations. And of the invasion of Iraq, which sharply increased terror in the West, confirming the predictions of British and American intelligence.

These acts of aggression were, again, a matter of little concern to planners, who are guided by altogether different concepts of security. Even instant destruction by nuclear weapons has never ranked high for state authorities—a topic for discussion in the next column.

THE PROSPECTS FOR SURVIVAL

March 31, 2014

THIS IS PART II OF AN ARTICLE ADAPTED FROM A LECTURE BY NOAM CHOMSKY ON FEBRUARY 28, SPONSORED BY THE NUCLEAR AGE PEACE FOUNDATION IN SANTA BARBARA, CALIFORNIA.

The previous article explored how security is a high priority for government planners: security, that is, for state power and its primary constituency, concentrated private power—all of which entails that official policy must be protected from public scrutiny.

In these terms, government actions fall in place as quite rational, including the rationality of collective suicide. Even instant destruction by nuclear weapons has never ranked high among the concerns of state authorities.

To cite an example from the late Cold War: In November 1983 the U.S.-led North Atlantic Treaty Organization (NATO) launched a military exercise designed to probe Russian air defenses, simulating air and naval attacks and even a nuclear alert.

These actions were undertaken at a very tense moment. Pershing II strategic missiles were being deployed in Europe. President Reagan, fresh from the "Evil Empire" speech, had announced the Strategic Defense Initiative, dubbed "Star Wars," which the Russians understood to be effectively a first-strike weapon—a standard interpretation of missile defense on all sides.

Naturally these actions caused great alarm in Russia, which, unlike the United States, was quite vulnerable and had repeatedly been invaded.

Newly released archives reveal that the danger was even

more severe than historians had previously assumed. The NATO exercise "almost became a prelude to a preventative [Russian] nuclear strike," according to an account last year by Dmitry Adamsky in the *JOURNAL OF STRATEGIC STUDIES*.

Nor was this the only close call. In September 1983, Russia's early-warning systems registered an incoming missile strike from the United States and sent the highest-level alert. The Soviet military protocol was to retaliate with a nuclear attack of its own.

The Soviet officer on duty, Stanislav Petrov, intuiting a false alarm, decided not to report the warnings to his superiors. Thanks to his dereliction of duty, we're alive to talk about the incident.

Security of the population was no more a high priority for Reagan planners than for their predecessors. Such heedlessness continues to the present, even putting aside the numerous near-catastrophic accidents, reviewed in a chilling new book, *COMMAND AND CONTROL: NUCLEAR WEAPONS, THE DAMASCUS ACCIDENT, AND THE ILLUSION OF SAFETY*, by Eric Schlosser.

It's hard to contest the conclusion of the last commander of the Strategic Air Command, General Lee Butler, that humanity has so far survived the nuclear age "by some combination of skill, luck and divine intervention, and I suspect the latter in greatest proportion."

The government's regular, easy acceptance of threats to survival is almost too extraordinary to capture in words.

In 1995, well after the Soviet Union had collapsed, the U.S. Strategic Command, or Stratcom, which is in charge of nuclear weapons, published a study, *ESSENTIALS OF POST–COLD WAR DETERRENCE*.

A central conclusion is that the United States must maintain the right of a nuclear first strike, even against non-nuclear states. Furthermore, nuclear weapons must always be available, because they "cast a shadow over any crisis or conflict."

Thus nuclear weapons are always used, just as you use a gun if you aim it but don't fire when robbing a store—a point that Daniel Ellsberg, who leaked the Pentagon Papers, has repeatedly stressed.

Stratcom goes on to advise that "planners should not be too rational about determining . . . what an adversary values," all of which must be targeted. "[I]t hurts to portray ourselves as too fully rational and cool-headed. . . . That the U.S. may become irrational and vindictive if its vital interests are attacked should be a part of the national persona we project to all adversaries."

It is "beneficial [for our strategic posture] that some elements may appear to be potentially 'out of control'"—and thus posing a constant threat of nuclear attack.

Not much in this document pertains to the obligation under the Non-Proliferation Treaty to make "good faith" efforts to eliminate the nuclear-weapon scourge from the earth. What resounds, rather, is an adaptation of Hilaire Belloc's famous 1898 couplet about the Maxim gun:

WHATEVER HAPPENS WE HAVE GOT,

THE ATOM BOMB AND THEY HAVE NOT.

Plans for the future are hardly promising. In December the Congressional Budget Office reported that the U.S. nuclear arsenal will cost $355 billion over the next decade. In January the James Martin Center for Nonproliferation Studies estimated that the United States would spend $1 trillion on the nuclear arsenal in the next 30 years.

And of course the United States is not alone in the arms race. As Butler observed, it is a near miracle that we have escaped destruction so far. The longer we tempt fate, the less likely it is that we can hope for divine intervention to perpetuate the miracle.

In the case of nuclear weapons, at least we know in principle how to overcome the threat of apocalypse: Eliminate them.

But another dire peril casts its shadow over any contemplation of the future—environmental disaster. It's not clear that there even is an escape, though the longer we delay, the more severe the threat becomes—and not in the distant future. The commitment of governments to the security of their populations is therefore clearly exhibited by how they address this issue.

Today the United States is crowing about "100 years of energy independence" as the country becomes "the Saudi Arabia of the next century"—very likely the final century of human civilization if current policies persist.

One might even take a speech of President Obama's two years ago in the oil town of Cushing, Oklahoma, to be an eloquent death-knell for the species.

He proclaimed with pride, to ample applause, "Now, under my administration, America is producing more oil today than at any time in the last eight years. That's important to know. Over the last three years, I've directed my administration to open up millions of acres for gas and oil exploration across 23 different states. We're opening up more than 75 percent of our potential oil resources offshore. We've quadrupled the number of operating rigs to a record high. We've added enough new oil and gas pipeline to encircle the Earth and then some."

The applause also reveals something about government commitment to security. Industry profits are sure to be secured as "producing more oil and gas here at home" will continue to be "a critical part" of energy strategy, as the president promised.

The corporate sector is carrying out major propaganda campaigns to convince the public that climate change, if happening at all, does not result from human activity. These efforts are aimed at overcoming the excessive rationality of the public, which continues to be concerned about the threats that scientists overwhelmingly regard as near-certain and ominous.

To put it bluntly, in the moral calculus of today's capitalism, a bigger bonus tomorrow outweighs the fate of one's grandchildren.

What are the prospects for survival then? They are not bright. But the achievements of those who have struggled for centuries for greater freedom and justice leave a legacy that can be taken up and carried forward—and must be, and soon, if hopes for decent survival are to be sustained. And nothing can tell us more eloquently what kind of creatures we are.

RED LINES IN UKRAINE AND ELSEWHERE

April 30, 2014

The current Ukraine crisis is serious and threatening, so much so that some commentators even compare it to the Cuban missile crisis of 1962.

Columnist Thanassis Cambanis summarizes the core issue succinctly in the *Boston Globe*: "[President Vladimir V.] Putin's annexation of the Crimea is a break in the order that America and its allies have come to rely on since the end of the Cold War— namely, one in which major powers only intervene militarily when they have an international consensus on their side, or failing that, when they're not crossing a rival power's red lines."

This era's most extreme international crime, the United States–United Kingdom invasion of Iraq, was therefore not a break in world order—because, after failing to gain international support, the aggressors didn't cross Russian or Chinese red lines.

In contrast, Putin's takeover of the Crimea and his ambitions in Ukraine cross American red lines. Therefore "Obama is focused on isolating Putin's Russia by cutting off its economic and political ties to the outside world, limiting its expansionist ambitions in its own neighborhood and effectively making it a pariah state," Peter Baker reports in the *New York Times*.

American red lines, in short, are firmly placed at Russia's borders. Therefore Russian ambitions "in its own neighborhood" violate world order and create crises.

The point generalizes. Other countries are sometimes allowed to have red lines—at their borders (where the United States' red lines are also located). But not Iraq, for example. Or Iran, which the United States continually threatens with attack ("no options are off the table").

Such threats violate not only the United Nations Charter but also the General Assembly resolution condemning Russia that the United States just signed. The resolution opened by stressing the U.N. Charter ban on "the threat or use of force" in international affairs.

The Cuban missile crisis also sharply revealed the great powers' red lines. The world came perilously close to nuclear war when President Kennedy rejected Premier Khrushchev's offer to end the crisis by simultaneous public withdrawal of Soviet missiles from Cuba and American missiles from Turkey. (The U.S. missiles were already scheduled to be replaced by far more lethal Polaris submarines, part of the massive system threatening Russia's destruction.)

In this case too, the United States' red lines were at Russia's borders, and that was accepted on all sides.

The U.S. invasion of Indochina, like the invasion of Iraq, crossed no red lines, nor have many other U.S. depredations worldwide. To repeat the crucial point: Adversaries are sometimes permitted to have red lines, but at their borders, where America's red lines are also located. If an adversary has "expansionist ambitions in its own neighborhood," crossing U.S. red lines, the world faces a crisis.

In the current issue of the Harvard-MIT journal *INTERNATIONAL SECURITY*, Oxford University professor Yuen Foong Khong explains that there is a "long (and bipartisan) tradition in American strategic thinking: Successive administrations have emphasized that a vital interest of the United States is to prevent a hostile hegemon from dominating any of the major regions of the world."

Furthermore, it is generally agreed that the United States must "maintain its predominance," because "it is U.S. hegemony that has upheld regional peace and stability"—the latter a term of art referring to subordination to U.S. demands.

As it happens, the world thinks differently and regards the United States as a "pariah state" and "the greatest threat to world peace," with no competitor even close in the polls. But what does the world know?

Khong's article concerns the crisis in Asia, caused by the rise of China, which is moving toward "economic primacy in Asia" and, like Russia, has "expansionist ambitions in its own neighborhood," thus crossing American red lines.

President Obama's recent Asia trip was to affirm the "long (and bipartisan) tradition," in diplomatic language.

The near-universal Western condemnation of Putin includes citing the "emotional address" in which he complained bitterly that the U.S. and its allies had "cheated us again and again, made decisions behind our back, presenting us with completed facts. With the expansion of NATO in the East, with the deployment of military infrastructure at our borders. They always told us the same thing: 'Well, this doesn't involve you.' "

Putin's complaints are factually accurate. When President Gorbachev accepted the unification of Germany as part of NATO—an astonishing concession in the light of history—there was a quid pro quo. Washington agreed that NATO would not move "one inch eastward," referring to East Germany.

The promise was immediately broken, and when Gorbachev complained, he was instructed that it was only a verbal promise, so without force.

President Clinton proceeded to expand NATO much farther to the east, to Russia's borders. Today there are calls to extend NATO even to Ukraine, deep into the historic Russian "neighborhood." But it "doesn't involve" the Russians, because its responsibility to "uphold peace and stability" requires that American red lines are at Russia's borders.

Russia's annexation of Crimea was an illegal act, in violation of international law and specific treaties. It's not easy to
find anything comparable in recent years—the Iraq invasion
is a vastly greater crime.

But one comparable example comes to mind: U.S. control of Guantánamo Bay in southeastern Cuba. Guantánamo
was wrested from Cuba at gunpoint in 1903 and not relin-
quished despite Cuba's demands ever since it attained independence in 1959.

To be sure, Russia has a far stronger case. Even apart
from strong internal support for the annexation, Crimea is
historically Russian; it has Russia's only warm-water port, the
home of Russia's fleet; and has enormous strategic significance. The United States has no claim at all to Guantánamo,
other than its monopoly of force.

One reason why the United States refuses to return
Guantánamo to Cuba, presumably, is that this is a major harbor and American control of the region severely hampers Cuban development. That has been a major U.S. policy goal for
50 years, including large-scale terror and economic warfare.

The United States claims that it is shocked by Cuban
human rights violations, overlooking the fact that the worst
such violations are in Guantánamo; that valid charges against
Cuba do not begin to compare with regular practices among
Washington's Latin American clients; and that Cuba has been
under severe, unremitting U.S. attack since its independence.

But none of this crosses anyone's red lines or causes a crisis. It falls into the category of the U.S. invasions of Indochina
and Iraq, the regular overthrow of parliamentary regimes and
installation of vicious dictatorships, and our hideous record of
other exercises of "upholding peace and stability."

EDWARD J. SNOWDEN, THE WORLD'S "MOST WANTED CRIMINAL"

May 30, 2014

In the past several months, we have been provided with instructive lessons on the nature of state power and the forces that drive state policy. And on a closely related matter, the subtle, differentiated concept of transparency.

The source of the instruction, of course, is the trove of documents about the National Security Agency surveillance system released by the courageous fighter for freedom, Edward J. Snowden, and expertly summarized and analyzed by his collaborator Glenn Greenwald in his new book, *No Place to Hide*.

The documents unveil a remarkable project to expose to state scrutiny vital information about every person who falls within the grasp of the colossus—in principle, every person linked to the modern electronic society.

Nothing so ambitious was imagined by the dystopian prophets of grim totalitarian worlds ahead.

It is of no slight import that the project is being executed in one of the freest countries in the world, and in radical violation of the U.S. Constitution's Bill of Rights, which protects citizens from "unreasonable searches and seizures," and guarantees the privacy of their "persons, houses, papers and effects."

Much as government lawyers may try, there is no way to reconcile these principles with the assault on the population revealed in the Snowden documents.

It is also well to remember that defense of the fundamental right to privacy helped spark the American Revolution. In the 18th century, the tyrant was the British government, which claimed the right to intrude freely into the homes and personal lives of American colonists. Today it is American citizens' own government that arrogates to itself this authority.

Britain retains the stance that drove the colonists to rebellion, though on a more restricted scale, as power has shifted in world affairs. The British government has called on the NSA "to analyse and retain any British citizens' mobile phone and fax numbers, emails and IP addresses, swept up by its dragnet," the *GUARDIAN* reports on documents provided by Snowden.

British citizens (like other international customers) will also doubtless be pleased to learn that the NSA routinely receives, or intercepts, routers, servers and other computer network devices exported from the United States so that it can implant surveillance tools, as Greenwald reports in his book.

As the colossus fulfills its visions, in principle every keystroke might be sent to President Obama's huge and expanding databases in Utah.

In other ways too, the constitutional lawyer in the White House seems determined to demolish the foundations of civil liberties. The principle of presumption of innocence, which dates back to the Magna Carta 800 years ago, has long been dismissed to oblivion.

Recently the *NEW YORK TIMES* reported the "anguish" of a federal judge who had to decide whether to allow the force-feeding of a Syrian prisoner who is on a hunger strike to protest his imprisonment.

No "anguish" was expressed over the fact that he has been held without trial for 12 years in Guantánamo Bay military prison, one of many victims of the leader of the Free World who claims the right to hold prisoners without charges and to subject them to torture.

These exposures lead us to inquire into state policy more generally and the factors that drive it. The received standard version is that the primary goal of policy is security and defense against enemies.

The doctrine at once suggests a few questions: Security for whom, and defense against which enemies? The answers are highlighted dramatically by the Snowden revelations.

Policy must assure the security of state authority and concentrations of domestic power and defend them from a frightening enemy: the domestic population, which can become a great danger if not controlled.

It has long been understood that information about the enemy makes a critical contribution to controlling it. In that regard, President Obama has a series of distinguished predecessors, though his contributions have reached unprecedented levels, as we have learned from the work of Snowden, Greenwald and a few others.

To defend state power and private economic power from the domestic enemy, those two entities must be concealed—while in sharp contrast, the enemy must be fully exposed to state authority.

The principle was lucidly explained by the policy intellectual Samuel P. Huntington, who instructed us that "power remains strong when it remains in the dark; exposed to the sunlight it begins to evaporate."

Huntington added a crucial illustration. In his words, "you may have to sell [intervention or other military action] in such a way as to create the misimpression that it is the Soviet Union that you are fighting. That is what the United States has been doing ever since the Truman Doctrine" at the outset of the Cold War.

Huntington's insight into state power and policy was both accurate and prescient. As he wrote these words in 1981, the Reagan administration was launching its war on terror—which quickly became a murderous and brutal terrorist war, primarily in Central America, but extending well beyond to southern Africa, Asia and the Middle East.

From that day forward, to carry out violence and subversion abroad, or repression and violation of fundamental rights at home, state power has regularly sought to create the misimpression that it is terrorists that you are fighting, though there are other options: drug lords, mad mullahs seeking nuclear weapons, and other ogres said to be seeking to attack and destroy us.

Throughout, the basic principle remains: Power must not be exposed to the sunlight. Edward Snowden has become the most wanted criminal in the world for failing to comprehend this essential maxim.

In brief, there must be complete transparency for the population, but none for the powers that must defend themselves from this fearsome internal enemy.

THE SLEDGEHAMMER WORLDVIEW
July 3, 2014

The front page of the *New York Times* on June 26 featured a photo of women mourning a murdered Iraqi.

He is one of the innumerable victims of the ISIS (Islamic State in Iraq and Syria) campaign in which the Iraqi army, armed and trained by the U.S. for many years, quickly melted away, abandoning much of Iraq to a few thousand militants, hardly a new experience in imperial history.

Right above the picture is the newspaper's famous motto: "All the News That's Fit to Print."

There is a crucial omission. The front page should display the words of the Nuremberg judgment of prominent Nazis—words that must be repeated until they penetrate general consciousness: Aggression is "the supreme international crime differing only from other war crimes in that it contains within itself the accumulated evil of the whole."

And alongside these words there should be the admonition of the chief prosecutor for the United States, Robert Jackson: "The record on which we judge these defendants is the record on which history will judge us tomorrow. To pass these defendants a poisoned chalice is to put it to our own lips as well."

The U.S.-U.K. invasion of Iraq was a textbook example of aggression. Apologists invoke noble intentions, which would be irrelevant even if the pleas were sustainable.

For the World War II tribunals, it mattered not a jot that Japanese imperialists were intent on bringing an "earthly paradise" to the Chinese they were slaughtering, or that Hitler sent troops into Poland in 1939 in self-defense against the "wild terror" of the Poles. The same holds when we sip from the poisoned chalice.

Those at the wrong end of the club have few illusions. Abdel Bari Atwan, editor of a Pan-Arab website, observes that "the main factor responsible for the current chaos [in Iraq] is the U.S./Western occupation and the Arab backing for it. Any other claim is misleading and aims to divert attention [away] from this truth."

In a recent interview with *MOYERS & COMPANY*, Iraq specialist Raed Jarrar outlines what we in the West should know. Like many Iraqis, he is half-Shiite, half-Sunni, and in pre-invasion Iraq he barely knew the religious identities of his relatives, because "sect wasn't really a part of the national consciousness."

Jarrar reminds us that "this sectarian strife that is destroying the country . . . clearly began with the U.S. invasion and occupation."

The aggressors destroyed "Iraqi national identity and replaced it with sectarian and ethnic identities," beginning immediately when the United States imposed a Governing Council based on sectarian identity, a novelty for Iraq.

By now, Shiites and Sunnis are the bitterest enemies, thanks to the sledgehammer wielded by Donald Rumsfeld and Dick Cheney (respectively the former U.S. Secretary of Defense and vice president during the George W. Bush administration) and others like them who understand nothing beyond violence and terror and have helped to create conflicts that are now tearing the region to shreds.

Other headlines report the resurgence of the Taliban in Afghanistan. Journalist Anand Gopal explains the reasons in his remarkable book, *NO GOOD MEN AMONG THE LIVING: AMERICA, THE TALIBAN, AND THE WAR THROUGH AFGHAN EYES.*

In 2001–2002, when the U.S. sledgehammer struck Afghanistan, the al-Qaida outsiders there soon disappeared and the Taliban melted away, many choosing in traditional style to accommodate to the latest conquerors.

But Washington was desperate to find terrorists to crush. The strongmen they imposed as rulers quickly discovered that they could exploit Washington's blind ignorance and attack their enemies, including those eagerly collaborating with the American invaders.

Soon the country was ruled by ruthless warlords, while many former Taliban who sought to join the new order recreated the insurgency.

The sledgehammer was later picked up by President Obama as he "led from behind" in smashing Libya.

In March 2011, amid an Arab Spring uprising against Libyan ruler Moammar Gadhafi, the U.N. Security Council passed Resolution 1973, calling for "a cease-fire and a complete end to violence and all attacks against, and abuses of, civilians."

The imperial triumvirate—France, England and the United States—instantly chose to violate the Resolution, becoming the air force of the rebels and sharply enhancing violence.

Their campaign culminated in the assault on Gadhafi's refuge in Sirte, which they left "utterly ravaged," "reminiscent of the grimmest scenes from Grozny, towards the end of Russia's bloody Chechen war," according to eyewitness reports in the British press. At a bloody cost, the triumvirate accomplished its goal of regime change in violation of pious pronouncements to the contrary.

The African Union strongly opposed the triumvirate assault. As reported by Africa specialist Alex de Waal in the British journal *INTERNATIONAL AFFAIRS*, the A.U. established a "road map" calling for cease-fire, humanitarian assistance, protection of African migrants (who were largely slaughtered or expelled) and other foreign nationals, and political reforms to eliminate "the causes of the current crisis," with further steps to establish "an inclusive, consensual interim government, leading to democratic elections."

The African Union's framework was accepted in principle by Gadhafi but dismissed by the triumvirate, who "were uninterested in real negotiations," de Waal observes.

The outcome is that Libya is now torn by warring militias, while jihadi terror has been unleashed in much of Africa along with a flood of weapons, reaching also to Syria.

There is plenty of evidence of the consequences of resort to the sledgehammer. Take the Democratic Republic of Congo, formerly the Belgian Congo, a huge country rich in resources—and one of the worst contemporary horror stories. It had a chance for successful development after independence in 1960, under the leadership of Prime Minister Patrice Lumumba.

But the West would have none of that. CIA head Allen Dulles determined that Lumumba's "removal must be an urgent and prime objective" of covert action, not least because U.S. investments might have been endangered by what internal documents refer to as "radical nationalists."

Under the supervision of Belgian officers, Lumumba was murdered, realizing President Eisenhower's wish that he "would fall into a river full of crocodiles." Congo was handed over to the U.S. favorite, the murderous and corrupt dictator Mobutu Sese Seko, and on to today's wreckage of Africa's hopes.

Closer to home it is harder to ignore the consequences of U.S. state terror. There is now great concern about the flood of children fleeing to the United States from Central America.

The *WASHINGTON POST* reports that the surge is "mostly from Guatemala, El Salvador and Honduras"—but not Nicaragua. Why? Could it be that when Washington's sledgehammer was battering the region in the 1980s, Nicaragua was the one country that had an army to defend the population from U.S.-run terrorists, while in the other three countries the terrorists devastating the countries were the armies equipped and trained by Washington?

Obama has proposed a humanitarian response to the tragic influx: more efficient deportation. Do alternatives come to mind?

It is unfair to omit exercises of "soft power" and the role of the private sector. A good example is Chevron's decision to abandon its widely touted renewable energy programs, because fossil fuels are far more profitable.

Exxon Mobil in turn announced "that its laserlike focus on fossil fuels is a sound strategy, regardless of climate change," *BLOOMBERG BUSINESSWEEK* reports, "because the world needs vastly more energy and the likelihood of significant carbon reductions is 'highly unlikely.'"

It is therefore a mistake to remind readers daily of the Nuremberg judgment. Aggression is no longer the "supreme international crime." It cannot compare with destruction of the lives of future generations to ensure bigger bonuses tomorrow.

NIGHTMARE IN GAZA

August 1, 2014

Amid all the horrors unfolding in the latest Israeli offensive in Gaza, Israel's goal is simple: quiet-for-quiet, a return to the norm.

For the West Bank, the norm is that Israel continues its illegal construction of settlements and infrastructure so that it can integrate into Israel whatever might be of value, meanwhile consigning Palestinians to unviable cantons and subjecting them to repression and violence.

For Gaza, the norm is a miserable existence under a cruel and destructive siege that Israel administers to permit bare survival but nothing more.

The latest Israeli rampage was set off by the brutal murder of three Israeli boys from a settler community in the occupied West Bank. A month before, two Palestinian boys were shot dead in the West Bank city of Ramallah. That elicited little attention, which is understandable, since it is routine.

"The institutionalized disregard for Palestinian life in the West helps explain not only why Palestinians resort to violence," Middle East analyst Mouin Rabbani reports, "but also Israel's latest assault on the Gaza Strip."

In an interview, human rights lawyer Raji Sourani, who has remained in Gaza through years of Israeli brutality and terror, said, "The most common sentence I heard when people began to talk about cease-fire: Everybody says it's better for all of us to die and not go back to the situation we used to have before this war. We don't want that again. We have no dignity, no pride; we are just soft targets, and we are very cheap. Either this situation really improves or it is better to just die. I am talking about intellectuals, academics, ordinary people: Everybody is saying that."

In January 2006, Palestinians committed a major crime: They voted the wrong way in a carefully monitored free election, handing control of Parliament to Hamas.

The media constantly intone that Hamas is dedicated to the destruction of Israel. In reality, Hamas leaders have repeatedly made it clear that Hamas would accept a two-state settlement in accord with the international consensus that has been blocked by the United States and Israel for 40 years.

In contrast, Israel is dedicated to the destruction of Palestine, apart from some occasional meaningless words, and is implementing that commitment.

The crime of the Palestinians in January 2006 was punished at once. The United States and Israel, with Europe shamefully trailing behind, imposed harsh sanctions on the errant population and Israel stepped up its violence.

The United States and Israel quickly initiated plans for a military coup to overthrow the elected government. When Hamas had the effrontery to foil the plans, the Israeli assaults and the siege became far more severe.

There should be no need to review again the dismal record since. The relentless siege and savage attacks are punctuated by episodes of "mowing the lawn," to borrow Israel's cheery expression for its periodic exercises in shooting fish in a pond as part of what it calls a "war of defense."

Once the lawn is mowed and the desperate population seeks to rebuild somehow from the devastation and the murders, there is a cease-fire agreement. The most recent cease-fire was established after Israel's October 2012 assault, called Operation Pillar of Defense.

Though Israel maintained its siege, Hamas observed the cease-fire, as Israel concedes. Matters changed in April of this year when Fatah and Hamas forged a unity agreement that established a new government of technocrats unaffiliated with either party.

Israel was naturally furious, all the more so when even the Obama administration joined the West in signaling approval. The unity agreement not only undercuts Israel's claim that it cannot negotiate with a divided Palestine but also threatens the long-term goal of dividing Gaza from the West Bank and pursuing its destructive policies in both regions.

Something had to be done, and an occasion arose on June 12, when the three Israeli boys were murdered in the West Bank. Early on, the Netanyahu government knew that they were dead, but pretended otherwise, which provided the opportunity to launch a rampage in the West Bank, targeting Hamas.

Prime Minister Benjamin Netanyahu claimed to have certain knowledge that Hamas was responsible. That too was a lie.

One of Israel's leading authorities on Hamas, Shlomi Eldar, reported almost at once that the killers very likely came from a dissident clan in Hebron that has long been a thorn in the side of Hamas. Eldar added that "I'm sure they didn't get any green light from the leadership of Hamas, they just thought it was the right time to act."

The 18-day rampage after the kidnapping, however, succeeded in undermining the feared unity government, and sharply increasing Israeli repression. Israel also conducted dozens of attacks in Gaza, killing five Hamas members on July 7.

Hamas finally reacted with its first rockets in 19 months, providing Israel with the pretext for Operation Protective Edge on July 8.

By July 31, around 1,400 Palestinians had been killed, mostly civilians, including hundreds of women and children.

And three Israeli civilians. Large areas of Gaza had been turned into rubble. Four hospitals had been attacked, each another war crime.

Israeli officials laud the humanity of what it calls "the most moral army in the world," which informs residents that their homes will be bombed. The practice is "sadism, sanctimoniously disguising itself as mercy," in the words of Israeli journalist Amira Hass: "A recorded message demanding hundreds of thousands of people leave their already targeted homes, for another place, equally dangerous, 10 kilometers away."

In fact, there is no place in the prison of Gaza safe from Israeli sadism, which may even exceed the terrible crimes of Operation Cast Lead in 2008–2009.

The hideous revelations elicited the usual reaction from the most moral president in the world, Barack Obama: great sympathy for Israelis, bitter condemnation of Hamas and calls for moderation on both sides.

When the current attacks are called off, Israel hopes to be free to pursue its criminal policies in the occupied territories without interference, and with the U.S. support it has enjoyed in the past.

Gazans will be free to return to the norm in their Israeli-run prison, while in the West Bank, Palestinians can watch in peace as Israel dismantles what remains of their possessions.

That is the likely outcome if the U.S. maintains its decisive and virtually unilateral support for Israeli crimes and its rejection of the long-standing international consensus on diplomatic settlement. But the future will be quite different if the U.S. withdraws that support.

In that case it would be possible to move toward the "enduring solution" in Gaza that U.S. Secretary of State John Kerry called for, eliciting hysterical condemnation in Israel because the phrase could be interpreted as calling for an end to Israel's siege and regular attacks. And—horror of horrors—the phrase might even be interpreted as calling for implementation of international law in the rest of the occupied territories.

Forty years ago Israel made the fateful decision to choose expansion over security, rejecting a full peace treaty offered by Egypt in return for evacuation from the occupied Egyptian Sinai, where Israel was initiating extensive settlement and development projects. Israel has adhered to that policy ever since.

If the United States decided to join the world, the impact would be great. Over and over, Israel has abandoned cherished plans when Washington has so demanded. Such are the relations of power between them.

Furthermore, Israel by now has little recourse, after having adopted policies that turned it from a country that was greatly admired to one that is feared and despised, policies it is pursuing with blind determination today in its march toward moral deterioration and possible ultimate destruction.

Could U.S. policy change? It's not impossible. Public opinion has shifted considerably in recent years, particularly among the young, and it cannot be completely ignored.

For some years there has been a good basis for public demands that Washington observe its own laws and cut off military aid to Israel. U.S. law requires that "no security assistance may be provided to any country the government of which engages in a consistent pattern of gross violations of internationally recognized human rights."

Israel most certainly is guilty of this consistent pattern, and has been for many years.

Sen. Patrick Leahy of Vermont, author of this provision of the law, has brought up its potential applicability to Israel in specific cases, and with a well-conducted educational, organizational and activist effort such initiatives could be pursued successively.

That could have a very significant impact in itself, while also providing a springboard for further actions to compel Washington to become part of "the international community" and to observe international law and norms.

Nothing could be more significant for the tragic Palestinian victims of many years of violence and repression.

THE OWL OF MINERVA
September 3, 2014

It is not pleasant to contemplate the thoughts that must be passing through the mind of the Owl of Minerva as the dusk falls and she undertakes the task of interpreting the era of human civilization, which may now be approaching its inglorious end.

The era opened almost 10,000 years ago in the Fertile Crescent, stretching from the lands of the Tigris and Euphrates, through Phoenicia on the eastern coast of the Mediterranean to the Nile Valley, and from there to Greece and beyond. What is happening in this region provides painful lessons on the depths to which the species can descend.

The land of the Tigris and Euphrates has been the scene of unspeakable horrors in recent years. The George W. Bush–Tony Blair aggression in 2003, which many Iraqis compared to the Mongol invasions of the 13th century, was yet another lethal blow. It destroyed much of what survived the Bill Clinton–driven U.N. sanctions on Iraq, condemned as "genocidal" by the distinguished diplomats Denis Halliday and Hans von Sponeck, who administered them before resigning in protest. Halliday and von Sponeck's devastating reports received the usual treatment accorded to unwanted facts.

One dreadful consequence of the U.S.-U.K. invasion is depicted in a *NEW YORK TIM*es "visual guide to the crisis in Iraq and Syria": the radical change of Baghdad from mixed neighborhoods in 2003 to today's sectarian enclaves trapped in bitter hatred. The conflicts ignited by the invasion have spread beyond and are now tearing the entire region to shreds.

Much of the Tigris-Euphrates area is in the hands of ISIS and its self-proclaimed Islamic State, a grim caricature of the extremist form of radical Islam that has its home in Saudi Arabia. Patrick Cockburn, a Middle East correspondent for the *INDEPENDENT* and one of the best-informed analysts of ISIS, describes it as "a very horrible, in many ways fascist organization, very sectarian, kills anybody who doesn't believe in their particular rigorous brand of Islam."

Cockburn also points out the contradiction in the Western reaction to the emergence of ISIS: efforts to stem its advance in Iraq along with others to undermine the group's major opponent in Syria, the brutal Bashar Assad regime. Meanwhile a major barrier to the spread of the ISIS plague to Lebanon is Hezbollah, a hated enemy of the U.S. and its Israeli ally. And to complicate the situation further, the U.S. and Iran now share a justified concern about the rise of the Islamic State, as do others in this highly conflicted region.

Egypt has plunged into some of its darkest days under a military dictatorship that continues to receive U.S. support. Egypt's fate was not written in the stars. For centuries, alternative paths have been quite feasible, and not infrequently, a heavy imperial hand has barred the way.

After the renewed horrors of the past few weeks it should be unnecessary to comment on what emanates from Jerusalem, in remote history considered a moral center.

Eighty years ago, Martin Heidegger extolled Nazi Germany as providing the best hope for rescuing the glorious civilization of the Greeks from the barbarians of the East and West. Today, German bankers are crushing Greece under an economic regime designed to maintain their wealth and power.

The likely end of the era of civilization is foreshadowed in a new draft report by the Intergovernmental Panel on Climate Change, the generally conservative monitor of what is happening to the physical world.

The report concludes that increasing greenhouse gas emissions risk "severe, pervasive and irreversible impacts for people and ecosystems" over the coming decades. The world is nearing the temperature when loss of the vast ice sheet over Greenland will be unstoppable. Along with melting Antarctic ice, that could raise sea levels to inundate major cities as well as coastal plains.

The era of civilization coincides closely with the geological epoch of the Holocene, beginning over 11,000 years ago. The previous Pleistocene epoch lasted 2.5 million years. Scientists now suggest that a new epoch began about 250 years ago, the Anthropocene, the period when human activity has had a dramatic impact on the physical world. The rate of change of geological epochs is hard to ignore.

One index of human impact is the extinction of species, now estimated to be at about the same rate as it was 65 million years ago when an asteroid hit the Earth. That is the presumed cause for the ending of the age of the dinosaurs, which opened the way for small mammals to proliferate, and ultimately modern humans. Today, it is humans who are the asteroid, condemning much of life to extinction.

The IPCC report reaffirms that the "vast majority" of known fuel reserves must be left in the ground to avert intolerable risks to future generations. Meanwhile the major energy corporations make no secret of their goal of exploiting these reserves and discovering new ones.

A day before its summary of the IPCC conclusions, the *New York Times* reported that huge Midwestern grain stocks are rotting so that the products of the North Dakota oil boom can be shipped by rail to Asia and Europe.

One of the most feared consequences of anthropogenic global warming is the thawing of permafrost regions. A study in *Science* magazine warns that "even slightly warmer temperatures [less than anticipated in coming years] could start melting permafrost, which in turn threatens to trigger the release of huge amounts of greenhouse gases trapped in ice," with possible "fatal consequences" for the global climate.

Arundhati Roy suggests that the "most appropriate metaphor for the insanity of our times" is the Siachen Glacier, where Indian and Pakistani soldiers have killed each other on the highest battlefield in the world. The glacier is now melting and revealing "thousands of empty artillery shells, empty fuel drums, ice axes, old boots, tents and every other kind of waste that thousands of warring human beings generate" in meaningless conflict. And as the glaciers melt, India and Pakistan face indescribable disaster.

Sad species. Poor Owl.

Index